THE U.S. NAVAL INSTITUTE ON

# NAVAL
# INNOVATION

## U.S. NAVAL INSTITUTE
### W H E E L   B O O K S

In the U.S. Navy, "Wheel Books" were once found in the uniform pockets of every junior and many senior petty officers. Each small notebook was unique to the Sailor carrying it, but all had in common a collection of data and wisdom that the individual deemed useful in the effective execution of his or her duties. Often used as a substitute for experience among neophytes and as a portable library of reference information for more experienced personnel, those weathered pages contained everything from the time of the next tide, to leadership hints from a respected chief petty officer, to the color coding of the phone-and-distance line used in underway replenishments.

In that same tradition, U.S. Naval Institute Wheel Books provide supplemental information, pragmatic advice, and cogent analysis on topics important to all naval professionals. Drawn from the U.S. Naval Institute's vast archives, the series combines articles from the Institute's flagship publication *Proceedings*, as well as selections from the oral history collection and from Naval Institute Press books, to create unique guides on a wide array of fundamental professional subjects.

THE U.S. NAVAL INSTITUTE ON

# NAVAL
# INNOVATION

EDITED BY JOHN E. JACKSON

NAVAL INSTITUTE PRESS
*Annapolis, Maryland*

Naval Institute Press
291 Wood Road
Annapolis, MD 21402

**Library of Congress Cataloging-in-Publication Data**
The U.S. Naval Institute on naval innovation / edited by Captain John E. Jackson,
USN (Ret.).
    pages cm. — (Wheel books)
  Includes bibliographical references and index.
  ISBN 978-1-61251-849-7 (alk. paper)
  1. United States. Navy—Officers' handbooks. 2. Naval art and science—
Technological innovations—United States. I. Jackson, John E., Captain.
  V133.U86 2015
  359'.070973—dc23
                                                        2015023424

♾ Print editions meet the requirements of ANSI/NISO z39.48–1992
(Permanence of Paper). Printed in the United States of America.

23  22  21  20  19  18  17  16  15      9  8  7  6  5  4  3  2  1
First printing

# CONTENTS

# EDITOR'S NOTE

**Because this book is an anthology,** containing documents from different time periods, the selections included here are subject to varying styles and conventions. Other variables are introduced by the evolving nature of the Naval Institute's publication practices. For those reasons, certain editorial decisions were required in order to avoid introducing confusion or inconsistencies and to expedite the process of assembling these sometimes disparate pieces.

## Gender

Most jarring of the differences that readers will encounter are likely those associated with gender. Many of the included selections were written when the armed forces were primarily a male domain and so adhere to purely masculine references. I have chosen to leave the original language intact in these documents for the sake of authenticity and to avoid the complications that can arise when trying to make anachronistic adjustments. So readers are asked to "translate" (converting the ubiquitous "he" to "he or she" and "his" to "her or his" as required) and, while doing so, to celebrate the progress that we have made in these matters in more recent times.

## Author "Biographies"

Another problem arises when considering biographical information of the various authors whose works make up this special collection. Some of the selections included in this anthology were originally accompanied by biographical information about their authors. Others were not. Those "biographies" that do exist vary a great deal in terms of length and depth, some amounting to a single sentence pertaining to the author's current duty station, others consisting of several paragraphs that cover the author's career. Varying degrees of research— some quite time consuming and some yielding no results—are required to find biographical information from other sources. Because of these uneven variables, and because as a general rule we are more interested in what these authors have to say more than who they are or were, I have chosen to even the playing field by foregoing accompanying "biographies." Relevant biographical information has been included in some of the accompanying commentaries, however.

## Ranks

I have retained the ranks of the authors *at the time of their publication.* As noted above, some of the authors wrote early in their careers, and the sagacity of their earlier contributions says much about the individuals, about the significance of the Naval Institute's forum, and about the importance of writing to the naval services—something that is sometimes underappreciated.

## Deletions

Most of the articles included here are intact, appearing as they originally did in their entirety, but in a few cases some portions have been removed because they make suggestions or challenge policies/programs that no longer exist. Where these deletions have occurred, the following has been inserted: […]

In the interest of space, and because Wheel Books are intended as professional guides, not academic treatises, citations have been removed from some of the entries.

## Other Anomalies

Readers may detect some inconsistencies in editorial style, reflecting staff changes at the Naval Institute, evolving practices in publishing itself, and various other factors not always identifiable. Some of the selections will include citational support, others will not. Authors sometimes coined their own words and occasionally violated traditional style conventions. *Bottom line:* with the exception of the removal of some extraneous materials (such as section numbers from book excerpts) and the conversion to a consistent font and overall design, these articles and excerpts appear as they originally did when first published.

# INTRODUCTION

In his classic treatise on power, *The Prince*, Niccolo Machiavelli succinctly defined the inherent difficulty in promoting change and innovation when he noted:

> [T]here is nothing more difficult to carry out, nor more doubtful of success, nor more dangerous to handle, than to initiate a new order of things. For the reformer has enemies in all those who profit by the old order and only lukewarm defenders in all those who would profit from the new order . . . (because of) the incredulity of mankind, who do not truly believe in anything new until they have had actual experience of it.[1]

The purpose of this Wheel Book is to consider how the sea services have dealt with innovation and change in the past, as illustrated by selected articles that have appeared in the various periodicals and books published by the U.S. Naval Institute. It will also address the outlook for accommodating change in the future. If readers expect this to be a "cookbook" with a detailed and tried-and-true recipe for innovation, however, I acknowledge at the outset that no such recipe exists. The value derived from these pages will arise from the thoughtful consideration and assessment of ideas expressed by other maritime professionals in the first decade-and-a-half of the twenty-first century. (Other books in the USNI Wheel Book series will take a more historical approach, and will delve into USNI archives going back more than 140 years.)

At the most fundamental level, our topic relates to the only constant in life: change! Were it not for change, yesterday's tactics and last year's equipment would be adequate to provide for the common defense. But factors such as changes in political alliances, upheavals in cultural relations, and technological breakthroughs virtually guarantee that the path forward will be different from the path that brought us to the status quo.

I write these thoughts while serving on the faculty of the historic Naval War College in Newport, Rhode Island. It has been well documented that the College's founding president, Rear Admiral Stephen B. Luce, USN, embraced the changes he was witnessing in the Navy (and the world) when he founded the College more than 130 years ago. These changes were acknowledged in John Hattendorf's centennial history of the College when he noted:

> In 1884, the United States Navy was in a period of transition which reflected the broad developments in American intellectual percep-tions, the growth of industrial power, technological progress, and gen-eral professional development. Change was in the air, and suggestions for future development were heard in many different areas.[2]

The issues facing today's maritime leaders are, perhaps, not quite as trans-formational as those of Luce's time, but I would argue that the *rate of change* is greater today than at any time in our history. As one tech-based example, the Apple iPhone first went on sale in 2007, and there have been seven updated replacement versions since then, an average of one per year. And in May of 2014, Apple sold its 500-millionth phone. Changes in other technologies, such as weapons systems or consumer electronics, and in culture—or even fashion— have moved at a similarly blistering pace. For this reason, I argue that this accelerated rate of change places a premium on adaptation and innovation in virtually every field.

Creative, innovative, and adaptive thinking is of particular importance today because of the highly fluid nature of world affairs. This period has been catego-rized by the acronym VUCA, a term developed at the U.S. Army War College in response to changes in the security environment over the last twenty years. The concept has garnered a wide following both inside and outside of government. The acronym represents the following characteristics of the modern world:

Volatility: the rate of change of the environment. Volatility in the Information Age means even the most current data may not provide an adequate context for decision-making. Beyond an ability to accurately assess the current environment, leaders must anticipate rapid change and do their best to predict what may happen within the time scope of a project, program, or operation. Volatility in the environment coupled with the extended timelines of modern acquisition programs creates a unique challenge for strategic leaders and their advisers.

Uncertainty: the inability to know everything about a situation and the difficulty of predicting the nature and effect of change (the nexus of uncertainty and volatility.) Uncertainty often delays decision-making processes and increases the likelihood of vastly divergent opinions about the future. It drives the need for intelligent risk management and hedging strategies.

Complexity: the difficulty of understanding the interactions between multiple parts or factors and of predicting the primary and subsequent effects of changing one or more factors in a highly interdependent system or even system of systems. Complexity differs from uncertainty; though it may be possible to predict immediate outcomes of single interactions within a broader web, the non-linear branches and sequels multiply so quickly and double back on previous connections so as to overwhelm most assessment processes. Complexity could be said to create uncertainty because of the sheer volume of possible interactions and outcomes.

Ambiguity: describes a specific type of uncertainty that results from differences in interpretation when contextual clues are insufficient to clarify meaning. Ironically, "ambiguous" is an ambiguous term, whose definition changes subtly depending on the context of its usage.

For our purposes here, it refers to the difficulty of interpreting meaning when context is blurred by factors such as cultural blindness, cognitive bias, or limited perspective. At the strategic level, leaders can often legitimately interpret events in more than one way, and the likelihood of misinterpretation is high.[3]

How, then, can innovation, creativity, and adaptability help us deal with the VUCA world? Innovation often focuses on hardware: in the previous century, it was submarines and carrier-launched aircraft; today it is directed energy, drones, and other scientific breakthroughs. But in reality, innovation is about a great deal more than hardware. Leaders, both in and out of the military, must have adaptive and agile minds, able to operate efficiently in spite of this level of near chaos. Developing open minds, willing and able to consider new ideas, is facilitated by formal education programs such as those offered at the Naval War College and other professional military education institutions; through self-directed exposure to the thoughts of others by participating in programs such as the Chief of Naval Operations Professional Reading Program (CNO-PRP); and through involvement with the numerous interest groups and blogs that have proliferated on the internet. Professional competency in one's chosen field is fundamental, but taking the next steps to expand your vision beyond your in-box is critical to becoming an innovator.

At this point, a few words about the nature of innovation are in order. As a baseline, it is interesting to note that a simple Google search on the term "innovation" delivers more than 127 million hits in less than a half-second! (The fact that you can access this level of information with a few keystrokes is itself remarkable evidence of innovation.) Much has been written on the subject, and one can find *some* consensus on the factors necessary to create an environment in which innovative and adaptive thinking can thrive. It has been suggested that in industry, government, academia, and in other fields, leaders should:

1. Stress the importance of creative thinking, and be open to new ideas.
2. Allocate time—"white-space" if you will—in busy schedules, to allow new ideas to arise.

3. Cross-fertilize: Encourage discussions between diverse individuals who may bring new insights based on their experiences. We should avoid talking only to people with similar backgrounds and training. We should seek to step outside of our comfort zone.

4. Tolerate mistakes and encourage mental "risk taking."

5. Reward creativity. Individuals with creative and adaptive minds are a valuable commodity and should be prized and protected.

6. Act on ideas. Great ideas and new concepts are only worthwhile if they result in action.

Hopefully these thoughts, consisting of just over one hundred words, provide some practical examples of steps we can take to foster innovation in whatever line of work we lead. The validity of these broad steps will be addressed in many of the articles reproduced in this Wheel Book.

Certainly, the process of encouraging innovation is not easy and there have always been impediments to change. Noted British military historian and theorist B. H. Liddell Hart is famously quoted as saying, "The only thing harder than getting a new idea into the military mind is to get an old one out."[4] I would argue that this sentiment applies equally to non-military minds, which are also conditioned by a lifetime of experiences to seek comfort in the familiar, and to remain cautious about the new and the unknown. Regardless of how difficult it may be, I argue that we *must be* innovative and adaptive if only because our enemies most certainly will be.

In addressing the subject of change, American historian and author Williamson Murray has noted:

It is clear that we live in an era of increasingly rapid technological change. The historical lesson is equally clear: U.S. military forces are going to have to place increasing emphasis on realistic innovation in peacetime and swift adaptation in combat. This will require leaders who understand war and its reality, as well as implications of technological change. Imagination and intellectual qualities will be as important as the specific technical details of war-making. The significant challenges here are how to inculcate those qualities widely in the officer corps and what are the peacetime metrics.[5]

Murray further stated:

It is all too easy to suggest that the American military needs to be more adaptive and imaginative in the twenty-first century. How to do so is the real question. Again, the answer is a simple matter, but its realization represents extraordinary difficulties because it involves changing military cultures that have evolved over the course of the past century. And cultural change in large organizations represents an effort akin to altering the course of an aircraft carrier.[6]

Innovation, from a military strategist's perspective, is the single greatest guarantor of success. Inability to innovate—especially in the modern world—is a guarantor of failure. Returning once again to Murray:

A crucial piece of the puzzle for successful adaptation lies in the willingness of senior military leaders to reach out to civilian experts beyond their narrowly focused military bureaucracies. No matter how expert senior officers may be in technical matters, they can rarely, if ever, be masters of the technological side of the equation. Thus, real openness to civilian expertise in the area of science and technology must form a crucial portion of the process of adaptation.[7]

Similar factors drive successful innovation in peacetime as drive successful adaptation in war. Both involve imagination and a willingness to change; both involve imagination as to the possibilities and potential for change; and both demand organizational cultures that encourage the upward flow of ideas and perceptions, as well as direction from above. Particularly important is the need for senior leaders to encourage their staff and subordinates to seek out new paths. Both involve intellectual understanding as well as instinct and action.[8]

Much has been written over the years trying to explain and rationalize the nature of military innovation. Some suggest that innovation is more likely to occur in times of peace, when resources (R&D funding and research time) may be more plentiful. Others argue that innovation and adaptation are more likely to succeed during combat, when the stakes are higher and immediate results can be measured through changes on the battlefield. There is no "right answer." In a similar manner, some researchers hold that innovation must come from a uniformed "maverick" able to push his ideas through unyielding bureaucracies and seniors in the chain-of-command, while others theorize that innovation must come from outside the armed services themselves, from civilian leaders in the executive and legislative branches of government. Again, there is no single "right answer" or clear path. Historical examples can be found to support each perspective, and some will be offered for consideration in the articles that follow.

Since the U.S. Naval Institute is, by design, the "Independent Forum of the Sea Services," this Wheel Book has an appropriately saltwater flavor. In recognition of this fact, mention should be made of the fact that in 2012, Chief of Naval Operations Admiral Jonathan Greenert, USN, in a desire to encourage creative thinking in the naval service, created the Chief of Naval Operations Rapid Innovation Cell (CRIC), which is hosted by the Navy Warfare Development Command (NWDC). According to an 11 September 2013 NWDC press release, the purpose of the CRIC is

to provide junior leaders with an opportunity to identify and rapidly field emerging technologies that address the Navy's most pressing challenges. The CRIC capitalizes on the unique perspective and familiarity that junior leaders possess regarding modern warfare, revolutionary ideas and disruptive technologies. Participation in the CRIC is a collateral duty that does not require a geographic relocation or release from one's present duty assignments. Each member proposes a project and upon acceptance, shepherds their project to completion. The new members will rotate into the CRIC as current members complete their projects and rotate out. CRIC members regularly meet with leading innovators in the government and civilian sector, and have access to flag-level sponsorship, funding, and a support staff dedicated to turning a member's vision into reality. Members generally commit about four days per month outside of their regular duties, participating in ideation events and managing their project. Because CRIC membership is project-based, length of membership depends on the duration of the individual's project but should not exceed 24 months.

CRIC members are provided with modest funding to research, demonstrate, and promote ideas with the potential to have "outsize impact" on the future Navy. The CRIC and similar initiatives hold promise as methods to encourage innovation in the sea services. You can learn more about the CRIC at https://www.facebook.com/navycric.

The need for innovation and adaptation is evident in the Navy/Marine Corps/Coast Guard, and also throughout the Department of Defense. In mid-November 2014, Defense Secretary Chuck Hagel announced the Defense Innovation Initiative as "a Department-wide initiative to pursue innovative ways to sustain and advance our military superiority for the 21st century and improve business operations throughout the Department." The letter establishing the initiative is included, for ready reference, as the final exhibit in this Wheel Book. One of the first steps taken in launching the initiative was the establishment of the Defense Innovation Marketplace (http://www.defenseinnovationmarket place.mil) as a clearinghouse and linking tool to connect industry, academia, the scientific and engineering communities, and the DoD workforce to one another for the purpose of exchanging ideas and concepts. While Pentagon initiatives often come and go, it is hoped that this "jump-start of innovative thinking" will result in significant improvements in the way America defends itself in the decades to come.

In the pages that follow this introduction you will find book chapters and articles addressing ways leaders can establish an environment where innovation has a chance to succeed; examples of adaptation successes and failures; and some creative ideas that could shape the Navy of the future. This Wheel Book is divided into four parts:

**PART I: The Innovation Imperative**, where we review some general thoughts about the impact that innovation and disruptive technology can have on operations in the maritime realm, and how change can be embraced and channeled for future success.

**PART II: The Unmanned Revolution**, in which we consider the impact that unmanned and robotic systems are having now and will likely have in greater measure in the near future. Many of these systems represent the types of disruptive technologies described by Harvard's Clayton Christenson: "Products based on disruptive technologies are typically cheaper, smaller, simpler, and frequently, more convenient to use."[9] The first generation of military robotics has already demonstrated that they meet many of these characteristics.

**PART III: CYBER, the Most Disruptive Technology**, wherein various authors reflect on the all-encompassing threats and opportunities represented by modern society's dependence on computer-controlled and cyber-linked networks.

**PART IV: Thoughts on Possible Futures**, where a few specific "outside-the-box" technologies are identified and briefly discussed.

The choice of the articles and chapters reproduced here was extremely difficult, and more than 180 articles published since the year 2000 were initially chosen for consideration. This volume of information speaks to the quality and breadth of discourse that takes place under Naval Institute auspices every year. While no anthology can be exhaustive on any given topic, we hope this compilation is comprehensive enough to engender thoughtful consideration of the subject and that it will spark the intellectual curiosity of the reader.

Change is in your future; how you deal with it is up to you!

## Notes

1. Niccolo Machiavelli, *The Prince* (New York: New American Library, 1952), 49–50.
2. John Hattendorf, *Sailors and Scholars* (Newport, RI: Naval War College Press, 1984), 8.

3. *Strategic Leadership Primer, 3rd Edition* (Carlisle, PA: United States Army War College, 2010), 11–12.

4. B. H. Liddell Hart, *Thoughts on War* (Gloucestershire, UK: Spellmount Publishers, LTD, 1944), 42.

5. Willliamson Murray, *Military Adaptation in War* (Alexandria, VA: Institute for Defense Analysis, Paper number P-4452, Chapter 8, 2009), 16.

6. Ibid., 26.

7. Ibid., 16.

8. Ibid., 4.

9. Clayton Christenson, *The Innovator's Dilemma* (New York: Harper's Business Review Press, 2013), xviii.

# PART I

## The Innovation Imperative

# 1 "INNOVATION: THE FATHER OF ALL NECESSITY"

(Selection from chapter 13 of *The Accidental Admiral: A Sailor Takes Command at NATO*)

ADM James Stavridis, USN (Ret.)

**Admiral James Stavridis, USN,** is widely recognized as one of the brightest military officers of his generation. He is an operator, a thinker, and a writer who has found ways to express his ideas in print throughout his extremely successful naval career. His reputation for trying new ideas and adapting old ones to meet the requirements of evolving situations are legendary. In this chapter from his recent book, Admiral Stavridis discusses the need for innovation, and some ways in which change can be accommodated within military organizations.

## "INNOVATION: THE FATHER OF ALL NECESSITY"

(Selection from chapter 13 of *The Accidental Admiral: A Sailor Takes Command at NATO*) by ADM James Stavridis, USN (Ret.) (Naval Institute Press, 2014): 156–66.

> The dogmas of the quiet past are inadequate to the stormy present. The occasion is piled high with difficulty, and we must rise with the occasion. As our case is new, so we must think anew and act anew. —*Abraham Lincoln*

During my years as the supreme allied commander at NATO I kept a sign on my desk visible to everyone who walked into the room. It was another quote from Lincoln: "Nearly all men can stand adversity; if you would test a man's character, give him power." This is a truism that applies not just in the military or politics but in every aspect of civil society, and indeed in our families.

I like that quote for a couple of reasons. First and foremost, it reminded me every day that jobs steeped in power come with a built-in responsibility to exercise it in responsible, honest, and transparent ways. Second, and more subtly, the quote conveyed to me the ever-present need to overcome the day-to-day challenges—the adversities of the moment that constantly press in on a leader in any truly significant job. And frankly, while most men (and women) can *stand* adversity, it takes a lot of iron in your soul to step up and actually *overcome* the challenges and succeed at accomplishing the tasks at hand. It has been my good fortune to work with a lot of men and women who did overcome the adversity. A central lesson I took away is the value of innovation in success; whether in the military, government, or business, there are valuable lessons here. Let me explain how I arrived at that conclusion.

The central question for any leader, whatever the size or shape of his or her organization, is how to overcome adversity. What are the leadership and management tools that matter the most? There are many candidates: teamwork, drive, determination, civility, alignment, presentational skills, and strategic com-munications, to name a few; the list of useful tools and skills goes on and on. All are important. But at the top of my list is *innovation*. This was not a sudden epiphany that came upon me like enlightenment came to Paul on the road to Tarsus. Indeed, I came to the view that innovation is the critical ingredient in overall organizational achievement relatively slowly over the course of a couple of decades.

As you start out in the military, there is an enormous and obvious premium placed on repetitive training in order to improve. If a military organization wants to "up its game," the normal prescription is lots and lots of practice, drills, and exercises. And of course this makes sense. To use a sports analogy, if you want a better jump shot, go out and shoot jump shots—thousands and thousands and thousands of them. Think of Larry Bird as a boy in his backyard in Indiana spending hour after hour shooting baskets. It works. Slowly. In that sense, many organizations—particularly military ones, with a predisposition for uniformity and conservative approaches, but also civilian and governmental enterprises—are seduced into regimes that focus almost entirely on repetitive training to improve.

But what if you added innovation to repetition?

Back to Larry Bird. How about new technology? Suppose he had been given a pair of brand-new, spring-loaded, light-yet-tough Nike Air Jordans. Would they have given the aspiring ballplayer that extra bounce, that modicum of support that could help improve his shots? You bet.

Or how about technique? What about a change in procedure, breaking the wrist in a more pronounced way, applying more backspin to the ball and a slightly higher arc, taking advantage of a "larger" target by a sharper angle of descent to the rim? Would that innovation in technique have a positive effect? Clearly it would.

The problem, of course, is that most organizations don't devote enough resources to the innovation part of their games, especially to *disruptive technologies* or *disruptive innovations*—technologies or ideas that essentially create a new market by changing a fundamental value equation, thus reshaping an existing marketplace, usually rapidly and somewhat unexpectedly. Clay Christenson, a noted thinker and writer about innovation, has repeatedly pointed out the need to find, evaluate, and embrace disruptive innovations and technologies—even when it is not obvious that their time has come.

An example of disruption would be the arrival of the telephone during the era of the telegraph. Telegraph lines already crisscrossed the country, and there were trained operators, delivery boys to run the messages, huge investments, and lots of profit in all that. Why would anyone want to have a telephone? But the technology enabled the innovation of real-time conversation, thus reshaping the marketplace for communication. Such marketplace innovation has occurred often through history and seems to be accelerating in the twenty-first century.

I began reading and learning about innovation seriously about twenty years ago, and the more I look at big organizations and how leaders manage them, the more I believe in the need for it. The most important approach to innovation I've employed over the years is the use of "innovation cells." This means simply carving out a few very bright and mildly untethered people from the organization and giving them the authority, resources, and above all the charter to find and try new ideas. I tried this first about fifteen years ago when I was a young captain at sea in command of a group of about a dozen destroyers. I had a good group of ship captains in command of the individual ships, but I saw no real innovators among them, so I asked each of the ship captains to propose a junior officer for my innovation cell. I did the same with the various aircraft squadrons that were part of my command. After interviewing all of the candidates, I chose five of them, attached them temporary duty to my staff, and told them to think about antisubmarine warfare and strikes at sea on enemy combatant ships.

"Your job is to make everyone upset with your crazy ideas," I told them. "And don't worry if most of your schemes fail. In fact, I expect most of them to fail. This is like baseball—if you're hitting .250, and one in four of your ideas bears some fruit, you're having a solid season. You hit on one in three and it's .333—a career year for almost any ballplayer. Anything better than that is a Hall of Fame year, which I'm not expecting (but it would be nice)." I gave them a small budget, the luxury of time to work on their ideas, and turned them loose.

Many of their ideas were goofy and unmanageable. I remember one proposal to use old fifty-gallon oil drums tied together to simulate submarines for target practice. They tried to attach unclassified communication devices to our military systems in ways that would have violated every element of policy and regulation on the books. And they had lots of other unworkable ideas.

But they also came up with several new ways to employ our detection systems in synergistic ways, fusing the data. This means taking input from various sensors—such as a radar, which uses electromagnetic radio waves to measure a physical object; a sonar, which uses sound waves to do the same; and infrared detectors, which measure heat—and merging them together to create a coherent location and picture of a target. We did this both at sea and on the ground in Andean and Central American jungles.

The team did some superb work using emerging technologies, including tiny unmanned air vehicles dubbed "wasps" and real-time translation devices that we called "phraselators." They also explored ways to attack very low radar cross-section high-speed patrol craft, an increasing threat in coastal warfare.

Above all, the innovation cell had a synergistic effect as people throughout my command—about three thousand folks in all—saw that the leadership valued (indeed demanded) innovation. People who were not part of the innovation cell started to talk about new ways of doing business as a matter of routine. Ideas were batted back and forth across the wardroom table and in the squadron ready rooms. It was an awakening of sorts. And of course we continued to do the basic blocking and tackling that comes with the job of military preparation. But by adding to our effort through innovation, we were able to bring our game up to a new level.

That experience made me a believer. In each of my subsequent jobs I set up an innovation cell of some sort and tried to encourage new ways of thinking, reading, writing, and sharing ideas on innovation.

For the military broadly, of course, all this came into sharp focus after 9/11 when we were suddenly confronted with a very new sort of opponent—essentially a network of opponents who were superb innovators. Gradually over the post-9/11 decade our own innovations began to kick in, and we were able to create new ways of thinking about conflict and the tools, techniques, and procedures necessary to construct our own networks (leveraging special operations forces); deploying new types of sensors (unmanned vehicles, especially armed drones); collecting intelligence through big data (the cyberworld); using existing platforms in new ways (intercontinental ballistic missile–launching submarines converted to Tomahawk cruise missile shooting platforms, large deck amphibious ships providing "lily pad" bases for special forces); describing and implementing new ways of looking at conflict through international law; and other innovations.

Indeed, after the 9/11 strikes on New York and Washington, it was clear that we—the military—needed to develop very new ways of thinking about conflict. I was asked by Adm. Vern Clark, the chief of naval operations, to stand up an innovation cell. We built Deep Blue (after the IBM chess-playing machine and also a play on words connoting the deep ocean) on the backbone of the Navy Operations Group, the small think tank that Rear Adm. Joe Sestak had created immediately after 9/11. Our job at Deep Blue was to come up with new ideas, forging them in the intensity of what we felt at the time was a new era of warfare.

Some of our ideas failed; for example, a "sea swap" to keep ships forward deployed and fly their crews back and forth—although the concept is getting a new look in view of today's more resource-constrained environment. We designed new types of combat groups (expeditionary strike groups) centered on large amphibious ships combined with destroyers and submarines, carrying drones and special operations forces. Another idea was to repackage communications using chat rooms, e-mail, and primitive versions of social networks to leverage lessons learned operationally. We looked at unmanned vehicles on the surface of the sea, below the ocean, and in the air. We created training simulators using off-the-shelf video games as bases. And Deep Blue also looked at the idea of the "expeditionary sailor," reflecting the fact that tens of thousands of sailors would soon be serving far from the sea in the deserts of Iraq and the mountains of Afghanistan. How to train, equip, and prepare them for duty like that? Innovation!

Around this time I attended a conference at which all the Navy flag officers were present. I was a newly minted one-star admiral heading up Deep Blue. It was a memorable meeting for a couple of reasons. At one point a vastly senior four-star admiral approached me during a coffee break. He was a naval aviator, and he was very displeased with the emphasis we were placing on drones and other unmanned air vehicles. His comments, in a nutshell, were that I was "standing into danger," as we say in the Navy, in a career sense. And being a typical aviator, he was not subtle. "Stavridis," he said, "your career is over unless you learn how to stay in your lane." That was fairly unsettling but not entirely unexpected. When I mentioned this to a senior surface officer, a three-star who was a mentor and leader in the community, his comment was, "You better trim your sails, Jim." Hardly reassuring.

The other memorable revelation at the all–flag officer conference was delivered by the CNO. He talked at length about a study of flag officer traits that he had commissioned by a well-regarded consulting firm specializing in leadership training. The results of that study were compared with those of similar studies of very senior executives in private industry. The Navy admirals scored very high in almost every desirable trait: leadership, organization, dedication, energy, alignment, and peer review. But there was an exception to this parade of good news: Navy admirals scored the lowest in . . . willingness to take career risk—essentially the willingness to try new things, to champion innovation and change. I found it extremely ironic that this group of admirals—all of whom had demonstrated extreme reserves of physical courage in flying high-performance aircraft, spending months at sea, and conducting dangerous special operations—were simply *afraid* to take the bureaucratic risks that come with innovation.

Despite these obvious indications that I was perhaps not in the mainstream with my colleagues in this regard, I continued to try to build my innovation cell and hoped for the best. After all, I had never planned to make it past lieutenant, so I was playing with house money. Luckily for me, the CNO was a fan of what we were doing at Deep Blue, and my career did not come to a screeching halt. Shortly thereafter I was sent back to sea, perhaps before I could annoy the entire senior leadership of the Navy.

My new carrier strike group command in Florida was an ideal position for me: back in my home state; away from the two big fleet concentration areas of Norfolk and San Diego, where plenty of senior admirals would have been watching me a little too closely; and in the middle of the first few years of the post-9/11 era. I set up the innovation cell and turned them loose. By this time, a spirit of innovation was actually beginning to take hold in the Navy, pushed by a new generation of young commanders facing operational challenges of a different sort.

We sailed to the Arabian Gulf with a major load of innovative gear and ideas to try, including a midsized unmanned surface boat, the Spartan Scout; the phraselator translation devices mentioned earlier; several types of unmanned air surveillance vehicles of various sizes; simulator software to train our tactical watch officers "in stride"; and a group of young junior officers we called "innovation fellows" who came to the flag staff with a ton of good ideas. Not all of it worked out; in fact, we probably batted around .300 or a little less. But we learned a great deal, we failed fast, and our partnerships with other organizations tasked with innovation (e.g., the Defense Advanced Research Projects Agency, or DARPA) were very productive.

By the time I got to my first four-star job at Southern Command in Miami a few years later I had a mini-network of bright, disruptive thinkers at my disposal. People such as Capt. Kevin Quarderer, call sign "Q," brought a fusion of technical and tactical acumen to the idea of innovation. Kevin had been with me on several innovation cells earlier in my career, and he held several advanced technology degrees as well as a true bent for challenging the given orthodoxy. He brought other thinkers on board, and we set out to use innovation to tackle the challenges of drug smuggling and hostage taking through the jungles of South and Central America. Among many other ideas, Kevin developed new detection systems that could at least partially "see through" the thick triple-canopy jungle by fusing several different sensor inputs—radar, heat seeking, and biological. We used a high-tech high-speed surface ship, the Stiletto, to literally run down the drug boats. I gave this innovation to my two-star Army general, Keith Huber, and he proved to be a pretty good sailor, using the Stiletto in lots of creative ways in shallow water that would have made a more traditional ship handler blanch.

We used commercial satellites to map the region and find anomalies as well as to respond after disasters such as fire and flooding so that we could sharpen our reactions. The innovation cell turned to business leaders and asked a group of them to function as a mock drug cartel and model for us the business case and transportation/logistic concepts that the actual cartels might be using—after all, business is business. That enabled us to essentially reverse-engineer the trafficking routes and methods and apply our resources to killing them. Some of what we did is highly classified, but I can say that our innovation techniques and ideas had a powerful impact on stopping narco-trafficking: we took down the largest levels ever recorded in 2006–9 using these innovations.

When I took on the job as SACEUR in 2009, I found myself in the middle of one of the most conventional and conservative organizations in the world: the North Atlantic Treaty Organization. Founded in the early 1950s, it remains steeped in tradition. The large and heavily bureaucratic structure at NATO headquarters in Brussels includes nearly four hundred standing committees ready to parse the smallest detail of any idea of change—and then usually block it. Every decision has to gain the approval of all twenty-eight NATO nations, a process described technically as consensus but more accurately depicted by picturing a steering wheel with twenty-eight pairs of hands on it. I knew that bringing innovation to NATO was going to be a supreme challenge.

Luckily, I quickly found a pair of very bright officers: Navy captain Jay Chesnut and Air Force colonel Pete Goldfein. Both were career aviators, but in smaller communities—Jay was an antisubmarine warfare expert flying the S-3 Viking, and Pete was a special forces aviator who flew a wide variety of very special small aircraft. They brought a sense of partnership with private sector entities as well as working closely with DARPA. Over the course of our time in NATO they were able to bring along several key innovations. The most interesting was a biological sensing system that could be used to detect humans moving through unmanned zones—highly useful in everything from counterterrorism to stopping human trafficking.

In the end, of course, innovation is not all about technology. Chesnut and Goldfein were also both instrumental, along with Cdr. Tesh Rao, an electronics warfare pilot, in redesigning the entire NATO command structure. I had been tasked by the secretary general to figure out how to reduce the size of the standing command structure—the many headquarters scattered around Europe and the world. It was big and unwieldy, including as it did more than 15,000 officers and enlisted staff members across 11 major headquarters. I wanted to reduce our size by at least 20 percent, and was willing to consider cuts up to about one-third. I turned to my innovation cell and brought in other collaborators from across the NATO enterprise. We considered using a contractor to examine solutions with us, but I have always shied away from bringing in "outside experts," which seems to me almost a contradiction in terms for a military organization—we have to be our own experts.

In order to bring this bureaucratic innovation home, I tried to build a shared sense of the value of change. Lots of the NATO nations wanted to reduce overhead and save money, and their ambassadors were amenable to some fairly radical redesigns. Other nations were more traditionally rooted in the defensive structure of the alliance (and liked having jobs for their top military officers), so

I offered them the allure of new technologies that could streamline our ability to respond to twenty-first-century challenges—not a sudden invasion of NATO from the East, but rather the endless crises of Afghanistan, Libya, the Balkans, piracy, Syria, and so on that kept popping up in small, fast, discrete firestorms.

In the end, my innovation cell brought together a new plan for redesigning the overall command structure, closing 6 of the 11 headquarters, and reducing manpower from 15,000 to just under 9,000 personnel "on watch" assigned to some headquarters at any given time. Not too bad, really, for an organization with three million men and women under arms and twenty-eight nations engaged. We sold the plan to the top leadership—not without arguments and pushback— and the secretary general moved it in the political sphere with the help of the ambassadors from the leading nations. Secretary of Defense Gates came in as the closer and delivered the product. We also added several smaller, lighter, faster command elements to balance the loss of the big headquarters. For example, we closed a major land force HQ, a large maritime HQ, and one of our two air defense HQs—but we added a very lethal special forces HQ, a lighter strike HQ, and added significant missile defense technology to the remaining air HQ. Essentially, we moved from the lingering Cold War structure into an organization better prepared for twenty-first-century conflict. It all worked out fairly well.

What do I take away from all these years of trying to build innovation?

First, it is crucial to recognize the importance of innovation and the value of change. Leaders should emphasize it at every turn, pointing out historical examples (both from broader society and from the organization's own history). For example, I often spoke about the post–World War I 1920s–30s period of naval innovation led by Billy Mitchell and other early pioneers of aviation at sea and on nascent aircraft carriers. They overcame the entrenched bureaucracy of battleships and essentially invented the U.S. Air Force. *Self-talk matters.* What we say about ourselves at every level in an organization—communicated through briefings to the team, Web sites, annual "state of the command" addresses, videos posted on YouTube, and personnel policies—constitutes the internal strategic communication. This is particularly important coming from the leadership. Self-talk about innovation can be worth its weight in gold.

Second, you have to work hard to find innovators. This is difficult. At NATO (and indeed earlier) I tried to mine the small and somewhat disadvantaged service communities; for example, people from aviation communities that were "going out of business" but previously had performed somewhat oddball missions: special forces pilots, electronic warfare operators, tactical communication platforms. Generally (and there are, of course, exceptions), people in the "mainstream communities" of high-performance fighters, Aegis missile defense ships, aircraft carriers, nuclear submarines, and so forth are less inclined to embrace change and innovation. Why? Because they are doing just fine in their careers given the high premium paid to them by the standing organization. Searching out the officers and enlisted personnel who are just a half beat off the music and don't always stay in their lane is a valuable exercise.

Third, the innovators must report directly to the top of the organization. Reports filtered to the top through intermediate levels are "dumbed down" to the lowest common denominator by the time they reach it. There will be institutional resistance to doing this. I can't count the number of times my front office team came to me with proposals to downsize, eliminate, or reassign the people and resources devoted to the innovation cells. This also means the organization's leader must find the time to take the innovation briefs, evaluate them and decide where to put emphasis, and then move the idea into the mainstream—where it will again encounter resistance because it was "not invented by the main staff." The imprimatur of the leader is crucial to keeping innovation alive in an organization.

Fourth, resource the innovators! This means carving out sufficient amounts of money, people, and time to allow your innovation cell to flourish. It does not mean *huge* levels of resources; for even very large organizations, a relatively small number of people (say a dozen) can achieve big throw weight. Deep Blue in the Navy, Checkmate in the Air Force, the Policy Planning Staff at the State Department, and Google Ideas within Google are all examples of this. In terms of money, the best approach is to encourage (and sometimes require) the innovation cell to reach out in entrepreneurial fashion and find "other people's money" to fund their ideas.

Fifth, reward them appropriately. This can range from cash and bonus awards for civilians to better evaluations and medals for military personnel. And again, this kind of message moves through the organization, and people begin to know that the leadership and the organization itself reward those who take the risks of innovation—despite their frequent failures.

And speaking of frequent failures, sixth, accept that many ideas will fail. Not every well you drill will be a gusher—but a handful of successful wildcat wells can make you rich. Encourage recognition of failure early in the process— the so-called fail fast approach that many corporations take today. Don't keep hammering away when something isn't working—move on to the next good idea.

Seventh, publicize successes in real time. This means up, out, and down: talking about the wins within your organization, as we did frequently at NATO; telling your bosses (in my case both the NATO secretary general and the U.S. secretary of defense) about them in weekly/monthly "innovation alerts"; and briefing subordinate commands about the good ideas (and encouraging them to use them) at command conferences, semiannual gatherings, and in annual reports such as the posture statement required to be submitted to Congress. The occasional blog post, social network tweet or post, and even articles in traditional journals all help.

Finally, recognize that there will be doubters, skeptics, naysayers, and the occasional ad hominem attack associated with trying to change things. For instance, I gave a talk at the 2012 TED Global Conference. TED—Technology, Entertainment, and Design—is an annual gathering of innovators who give eighteen-minute talks on "the idea of their life." My subject was open source security: trying to create security in the turbulent twenty-first century through a fusion of international, interagency, private-public, and strategic communications in a "smart power" approach. I've received plenty of positive feedback, but the hundreds of thousands of hits have also included lots of "this will never work" and "who the hell is this guy and why is he so foolish and naïve."

Jonathan Swift, the great satirist, lampooned those who sail against the wind by depicting them as believing that "so shall ye know a genius is among you: there will be a confederacy of dunces allied against him." I am far from a genius, and those disagreeing with me are seldom dunces, but I am willing to suffer the slings and arrows of public criticism to champion the occasional disruptive innovation or technology.

In the end, much of human progress comes because of people who could never quite stay in their lane, as annoying as they can be. The trick, as always, is balance: find the way to maintain the value of current innovations and technologies, resource the disruptive possibilities, understand how the value proposition changes, analyze the market, and then bring the new online while gracefully removing the old. Of course it doesn't always go smoothly. As in mountain climbing, it is good to have a firm grip on the next rock before you completely let go of the one you have. But to get up the mountain you have to climb, not just cling to a couple of rocks. And remember that the top of the mountain is where the strongest winds blow.

# 2 "A TIME TO INNOVATE, A TIME TO STEAL"

LT Scott Cheney-Peters, USNR

**Lieutenant Cheney-Peters** is a surface warfare officer in the U.S. Naval Reserve. In this article, he advocates that leaders should be willing to ignore the "not-invented-here syndrome" and willingly borrow (or *steal*) ideas that have worked elsewhere. He believes that, without shame or regret, they should avoid "re-inventing the wheel" and capitalize on the innovations of others.

## "A TIME TO INNOVATE, A TIME TO STEAL"

By LT Scott Cheney-Peters, USNR, U.S. Naval Institute *Proceedings* (July 2014): 78–80.

At a meeting of the Disruptive Thinkers group in the summer of 2013, attendees were asked to name the most innovative military leader they knew. I have to admit, I was stumped. Others produced tales of front-line leaders developing creative solutions to near-insurmountable obstacles. The only answer I could immediately conjure was Lieutenant Commander Thomas Dodge, Kelsey Grammar's submarine commander in the movie *Down Periscope*, who, among other exploits, disguised his World War II–era diesel electric boat as a fishing vessel—complete with drunken strains of "Louie, Louie"—to avoid detection by a Navy patrol.

My inability to name a real-life Lieutenant Commander Dodge wasn't because I have known no great leaders. In my naval service I have encountered outstanding leaders—male and female, officer and enlisted—but no particularly innovative ones. This apparent disconnect is all the more perplexing given the recent emphasis on developing a culture of innovation in the Navy. The truth is a good leader does not need to be innovative, and an innovative leader is not necessarily a good one.

It is important to define "innovative" as a leadership trait. An innovative leader develops new methods and solutions to tasks and problems. This is an admirable characteristic, and one the Navy needs within its ranks. However, the Navy is best served when the burden of innovation does not fall to the leaders of its front-line operational units. Quite simply, the time and energy they spend developing original solutions to problems would be wasted if an effective answer already exists. Instead, the Navy should encourage these leaders to "steal" what works best until something better—and proven—comes along.

## Good Leaders Innovate; Great Leaders Steal

A leader adept at stealing requires an awareness of existing solutions, receptiveness to others' ideas, and the humility to adopt methods that are not one's own. The aim is to reduce duplication and extra work—not only for leaders, but also for those they lead. From shipboard instructions to training-team scenarios, great leaders know how to copy what works and are willing to do so, liberally dispensing credit as they go. They also require keen judgment: to determine the methods worth taking, to identify those most applicable to the situation at hand, and to know when to ditch the stolen goods for something better.

At the same time, no two situations, and therefore no two problem sets, are identical. Nor can any method or solution, such as a ship's force protection plan, hope to cover every conceivable scenario. To deal with a steady stream of new situations, it would appear at first glance that good leaders must be innovative. For example, a unique pier set-up might prevent the deployment of jersey barriers as required by the force protection plan. When such a seemingly original situation is broken down into its fundamental parts, however, few truly new elements emerge. While the force protection plan as written might not incorporate the pier set-up, adhering to the force protection principle of distance suggests implementing something else to separate the ship from potential threats. Here again a great front-line leader acts as a thief, aware of others' "jewels"—existing solutions and approaches to this more generic problem of creating separation—and intelligent enough to know which to grab in the circumstances. Granted, an innovative operational leader might come up with an interesting approach to the composite issue, and the trait would indeed be useful for truly new and unanticipated needs. In the great majority of situations, however, the operational leader is better off copying another's work because it is already known to be effective, or applying proven principles to address the component parts of a problem.

In the midst of the response to November 2013's super typhoon Haiyan/ Yolanda, the U.S. Navy faced the challenge of quickly and simultaneously filling multiple water containers. Hull maintenance technicians (HTs) on board the USS *George Washington* (CVN-73) used their ingenuity to devise a system they called "the Octopus" by welding together water distribution piping that could fill up to eight containers at once with fresh water. Upon completion it was flown to a shore location to aid in assistance efforts.[1]

This story was heralded as a model of Fleet innovation on the fly, yet observers noted that a similar need and set of solutions arose during previous U.S. Navy disaster-response efforts. For example, during the relief operations after the January 2010 earthquake in Haiti, HTs on board the USS *Carl Vinson* (CVN-70) built two 12-faucet fresh-water dispensers.[2] While the similarities should not detract from the innovativeness of the *George Washington*'s crew, they were denied an opportunity to consider the experience of their counterparts and had to spend time "re-inventing the wheel" with the real possibility of not meeting their objective. The anecdote also illustrates what Rear Admiral Scott Jerabeck meant when remarking that the Navy has lessons logged, not lessons learned, and the failures of its current infrastructure for capturing, validating, and disseminating those lessons.[3]

## A History of Thievery

The Navy must do two things to support thievery in the Fleet. First, it needs to inculcate a spirit of humility and receptiveness among operational leaders toward ideas that are not their own. Training should focus on breaking problems into their component parts and on the methods for finding and selecting something worth stealing, applying it, and determining when to ditch it.

Second, the Navy must ensure that organizational infrastructure supports this type of leader. The Navy needs a centralized, well-publicized den of thieves, a place where those in search of answers can find and copy from those who have already done the work of testing and validating an approach. A leader can't steal existing solutions they don't have access to or can't locate across fragmented individual databases.

The Navy has long supported thievery, from the study of naval history and broad military principles to attempts to capture lessons learned on the operation of specific weapon systems. Deckplate gouge is a time-honored example of informal attempts to pass on solutions, but technology offers the possibility of leveraging informal networks to do more. The Navy has begun pursuing internet crowd-sourcing efforts such as Massively Multiplayer Online Wargames Leveraging the Internet and the CNO's Reducing Administrative Distractions website.[4] In fact, many ideas on the latter site centered on the desire to make this form of information swapping and locating easier.

Whatever form this infrastructure takes, it needs more than just thieves. For front-line leaders to focus on applying proven approaches developed elsewhere, there has to be an "elsewhere" that focuses on developing the approaches. While this has traditionally taken the form of experts and academics in development groups, schools, and research facilities, it is increasingly the province of volunteers on the internet. Innovators are also needed to mitigate predictability—one of the dangers of using only the best approaches, especially as applied to tactics against an enemy—by generating multiple validated approaches and keeping new ones on file in case those in use lose their utility.

Conversely, innovators need feedback. This means that operational leaders at times need to validate innovation or provide a point of departure for innovators to refine. Communication is crucial in this partnership, including an awareness of the range of resources—or lack thereof—front-line leaders have at their disposal.

Having developed, tested, or validated an approach—whether original or stolen—the best leaders freely encourage dissemination of their findings. Richard Gallagher, author of a book on workplace leadership, believes that people gain more leadership credentials by encouraging others to spread their ideas than by squabbling over credit. "When you openly encourage people to steal your ideas and get in the habit of stealing from others and crediting them, wonderful things happen to your career that you could never imagine when you try to be the lone ranger with a great idea," Gallagher says.[5] Here the Navy's role is to provide efficient infrastructure for that dissemination so that it's easy to find and see.

The Navy is trying to sustain its commitments with less resources, a situation that typically equates to less time for front-line leaders. They have less time to practice and perfect their mission areas, less time to meet their operational requirements, and less time to lead. To succeed, they must steep themselves in the art of stealing to obtain tested means to achieve their objectives. They need to know that they don't have to create everything from scratch themselves, and the Navy must support their efforts with training and infrastructure.

Good leaders and innovators, while distinct, are interdependent. Good leaders need innovators to develop the methods, the tactics, and even the administrative forms they steal. Yet while feedback and innovation from the Fleet are always welcome, the Navy should not emphasize it as the focal point of development. Innovation must exist to support operational leaders, not vice versa.

It is better for an operational leader to copy than create, to steal rather than innovate. By doing so they are more likely to have the time—and the proven tools—to succeed.

## Notes

1. MC3 Peter Burghart, "George Washington HTs Pump Out Aid," www.navy .mil/submit/display.asp?story_id=77655, 15 November 2013.

2. MC3 Shentel M. Yarnell and MCSN Heather Roe, "Carl Vinson Sends Desperately Needed Water Ashore," www.navy.mil/submit/display.asp?story_id=50661, 20 January 2010.

3. RADM Scott Jerabeck, Lecture at Surface Navy Association, Hampton Roads Chapter Lunch, Hampton Roads, VA, 20 November 2013.

4. Massively Multiplayer Online Wargame Leveraging the Internet: Wargames run by the U.S. Naval Postgraduate School. Campaign now concluded, formerly at http://navyrad.ideascale.com/a/pages/about.

5. Rachel Zupek, "When a Co-worker Steals an Idea," CareerBuilder.com, http://msn.empleoscb.com/CBMiniSite/SharedPages/PrinterFriendlyArticle.aspx?articleID=395.

# 3 "RECAPTURING OUR CREATIVE DNA"

RADM Terry B. Kraft, USN

When this article was originally published, Rear Admiral Kraft was serving as Commander, Navy Warfare Development Command (NWDC), a forward-focused Navy unit dedicated to regaining what he calls the Navy's "innovation advantage." In this piece, Kraft provides some of his thoughts about the art and science of innovation and adaptation and calls for more operational exercises and war games. He speaks to the modern world's incredible rate of change when he states: "Mankind is in the midst of explosive leaps in the formulation of new ideas and opportunities."

## "RECAPTURING OUR CREATIVE DNA"

By RADM Terry B. Kraft, USN, U.S. Naval Institute *Proceedings* (April 2013): 46–51.

The current strategic and economic climate demands that the nation's armed forces look for innovative ways of preparing to fight wars. The Navy and Marine Corps are no exceptions.

Mankind is in the midst of explosive leaps in the formulation of new ideas and opportunities. The speed and reach of information systems have radically transformed the temporal and spatial dimensions of war. Intertwined by the Internet and social networks, previously unconnected ideas are being fused and transformed into reality at an astonishing rate. Despite this dynamic environment, much of the Navy remains shackled to cumbersome processes and outdated thinking. To exploit the era's rich atmosphere of ideas, and prepare for challenges that come with it, we must energize and capitalize on the enterprising nature and resourcefulness of our maritime professionals. The transition will involve creating a channel for new ideas while encouraging a participatory system of idea-generating, collaborative professionals.

As we look over the horizon, we must ensure that our naval fighting capabilities are agile enough to respond to rapid changes in the future operating environment. Here, we examine the role of innovation as the Navy and Marine Corps enter a new era of information-intensive warfare. What role does innovation play in shaping future capabilities? What conditions are important to generate and exploit innovative ideas? How do we instill a culture that promotes bold, creative thinking? To position our naval forces for success in the future we must find solutions that address these questions.

## What Is Innovation?

The first question to be answered is "what's in it for us?" Innovation is defined as creativity applied to a purpose to realize value. Innovation expert John Kao goes a little deeper in his "Innovation Manifesto."

> Innovation enables people to adapt to the waves of disruptive change . . . and the rate is increasing. Changes are brought about by new demographic and geopolitical shifts [and] by new and emerging technologies. The complexity of change is beyond most strategic planning.[1]

Innovation as applied to military science encourages creativity and original thought to realize value. Technological advances are occurring in abundance in the private sector. The challenge before us—better yet, the opportunity—is to closely follow and rapidly incorporate applicable new technologies. How well the Navy is able to do this may well determine its ability to move forward in the information age.

Kao goes on to state: "Creating what is both new and valuable—is not a narrowly defined, technical area of competence . . . rather, innovation emerges when different bodies of knowledge, perspectives and disciplines are brought together."[2] Our challenge is to develop a cooperative structure to enhance innovation while not crushing it with bureaucracy.

In his book *The Medici Effect,* Frans Johansson discusses the power of combining two seemingly unrelated fields to produce new ways of tackling old problems. The result is called an "intersectional idea." His view is that, to truly move in a new direction, it is important to "live at the intersection."[3] One community decided to give it a try. Commander, Submarine Forces sponsored the TANG Forum in November 2011. The effort brought together a diverse set of attendees, none above the rank of lieutenant, to generate a multitude of ideas centering on implementing new technologies for the submarine force. Regarding the outputs of the conference, then-Vice Admiral John Richardson commented:

> This was a landmark event for us. For the first time, we really harnessed the creativity and innovative spirit of our young operators, who are perfectly positioned in the intellectual "sweet spot"—they know our problem set in detail, and they are familiar with the intuitive interfaces from their gaming, smart phones, and tablets. The conference was so rich, some of the ideas were so mature, we'll be incorporating them into our next version of software updates in the next two years. Some were so powerful and sweeping, they will require bigger design changes in future blocks of *Virginia* SSNs [nuclear-powered attack submarines] and the new SSBN [nuclear-powered ballistic-missile submarine] class. We're also looking to expand this approach to other submarine problems.

## Innovation in Naval History

History offers a priceless cache of previously purchased lessons to those who will mine it and apply it forward. The Navy of the interwar years and early Cold War periods faced mesmerizing opportunities and challenges similar to those we face today. We must heed their lessons and adopt their innovative zeal to gain advantages in future operating environments.

The period of 1919–39, known as the interwar years, provides a fascinating glimpse at how innovation emerges in challenging environments. The primary constraint of that time was the Washington Naval Treaty that among other things limited the production of battleships and undercut forward-basing options. To overcome those challenges war planners began to think creatively. In building "War Plan Orange," Navy planners unleashed a torrent of new ideas, such as options for aircraft carrier use, long-range logistics at sea and floating drydocks.

To keep pace with the surge in new ways to prepare for conflict at sea, Navy leadership created the General Board which, as author John T. Kuehn notes, "was the locus where treaty preparation, building policy, and war planning all intersected. The board addressed strategy, the recommendations of the bureaus, policy-making, NWC [Naval War College] wargaming results and studies."[4] The board helped cut through the complexities and uncertainties of the day. It focused innovation by defining the problems, and its largely untethered efforts resulted in the advance of amphibious warfare, carrier aviation, and the formation of a complex campaign of "island hopping," as leaders considered how they would seize and hold new bases across the vast distances of the Pacific. Their efforts culminated in a clearly defined experimentation and wargaming process that yielded significant results. Fleet Admiral Chester Nimitz was to later remark: "The wargames with Japan had been enacted in the game rooms at the War College by so many people . . . that nothing that happened during the war was a surprise—absolutely nothing except the kamikaze tactics towards the end of the war."[5]

## Embracing Change

Before zeroing in on the future, it is important to look at how we currently innovate. Today, the U.S. military is just a small slice of the global industrial complex and as such is no longer in a position to keep pace with the creation of cutting-edge technology. What's more, attempts to "in-source" new ideas and concepts face the bureaucracy of the acquisition process, the influence of Congress, and the size and focus of Navy staffs. These things tend to stifle the generation and development of new ideas and concepts. The current configuration of the military was largely shaped by the Goldwater-Nichols Act of 1986. That legislation shifted power to the combatant commanders, all of whom have a very real need to meet the demands of their theaters on a daily basis. Much of this contributes to what many have called a "lethargy of the mind" when thinking about innovation in the Navy.[6]

Like the interwar years, we need a clear understanding of the issues we face. Theoretical physicist Albert Einstein said, "If I had an hour to save the world, I would spend 55 minutes defining the problem and five minutes finding solutions." John Kao describes this as an "Innovation Audit"—understanding what we have and what we need.[7] The first part is easy, the second more difficult. In defining "needs," the pattern today is to default to *things*—weapon systems and other material items that can fill a perceived capability gap. Now, more than ever, it is essential to recognize that innovation is much more than technical—it involves broadly questioning how we will organize and execute warfare in future environments. For the Navy, it means thinking, again, about being *challenged at sea.*

In 2011, senior military leaders, academic experts, and industry representatives converged in Norfolk, Virginia, to spend two days discussing the state of innovation as it relates to our maritime forces. The audience included leaders from all sea services and the joint world. The large local audience was nearly doubled by participants on Defense Connect Online. The purpose of the conference was to begin a larger campaign to reinvigorate the conditions for an innovative culture and overcome our internal barriers to innovation. Admiral

John Harvey, Commander of U.S. Fleet Forces Command at the time, made his views clear:

> The organizations and processes we use are purposefully designed to maintain course and speed—not to allow significant change. Most of what I have seen regarding innovation in our Navy has been activity driven, more focused on getting a program through another step in the process than solving real problems. Our choice is simple. We can either innovate today, or be forced to rapidly adapt in the middle of conflict.[8]

With the tone and expectations set, the forum concentrated on three lines of discussion: (1) We would need to create conditions conducive to innovation; (2) we would need to identify the type of problems to be addressed; and (3) we would need a channel to develop innovative ideas and concepts.

The issues discussed at the conference are not exclusive to the Navy. At a recent Naval Institute/Armed Forces Communications and Electronics Association Joint Warfighting Conference, retired Air Force Lieutenant General David Deptula commented that the biggest challenge we face as a military has nothing to do with any particular weapon system, nor is it programmatic or budgetary. "Our biggest challenge will be to overcome organizational inertia, open our minds, and get out of the box." Concepts such as Air-Sea Battle are good starting points to define future capabilities, yet they will need to avoid the seemingly inevitable descent into a shopping list—especially in today's austere environment. Instead, it is important to ask deeper questions that could spawn a more innovative examination of future issues.

Looking ahead, to move innovation from a cerebral activity to a *practice* will require a dispassionate review of how we currently organize, train, and equip our forces. The general theme remains: Future battles will be fought in the context of being *challenged at sea*. The following questions may help frame how we think about our future:

- Do we train our forces against a thinking opponent? The central piece of maritime power projection remains the carrier strike group (CSG). The incredible range, lethality, and flexibility of the CSG are undeniable. The process of preparing these forces for deployment is a well-defined, qualification-driven process resulting in a high state of readiness for the group. The question is, are we building real tactical capabilities in our main battery or just preparing them for the most likely day-to-day operations they currently face? We need to develop a thinking "red cell" that can use a wide array of capabilities to create new and different high-end scenarios.

- Wargaming is another area ripe for examination. Is our approach on target? During the interwar years, wargaming was a major venue for vetting innovative ideas and discovering new ones. These games were played at the Naval War College pitting flag officers against each other in scenarios mainly focused on the Pacific. Debriefs were detailed and often brutal. As we begin to look at future challenges across multiple domains, the value of operational-level wargaming could be significant.

- Where do integrated tactics live? A large part of responding to challenges at sea will be new and innovative tactics. While plenty of organizations are developing concepts of operation in the important areas of antisubmarine warfare, integrated air and missile defense, and power projection, little attention is being paid to how we will integrate these efforts in the future battle space. Incorporating disparate sets of tactics into our warfighting whole should be a key area of any innovation effort. The challenge may be to successfully integrate platforms and procedures to fight in higher-end environments across multiple domains.

- Are we training our commanding officers to have the personal initiative to succeed in future environments? The ability to execute while cut off from higher authority is often a key to victory on the battlefield. The Army and Marine Corps have begun to empower their leaders through "Mission Command."

In a recently published paper on the topic, Chairman of the Joint Chiefs of Staff General Martin Dempsey noted:

> In its highest state, shared context and understanding is implicit and intuitive between hierarchal and lateral echelons of command, enabling decentralized and distributed formations to perform as if they were centrally coordinated. When achieved, these practices result in decentralized formal decision-making throughout the force, leading implicitly to the opportunity to gain advantageous operational tempo over our adversaries.[9]

## Harnessing Our Talent

Becoming more innovative will require us to chart a new way to energize and channel ideas to higher echelons. It remains profoundly difficult for large-scale formal organizations, which prize stability, continuity, and predictability, to establish and maintain within themselves the organizational conditions required for research and creativity. Considering samples from the business world can help the Navy understand how to establish a process for moving forward. The key will be to step away from capabilities and acquisition thinking (things) and look across the scope of thought at new ways to operate in challenging environments. It will require harnessing different perspectives, both from inside and outside the military. It means regaining our innovative DNA.

The Navy is at a critical nexus. After a decade of operations in U.S. Central Command, the Navy and Marine Corps are filled with veterans who have tasted the challenges of combat and are ready to put their lessons to use for the greater good. As one junior officer noted a year ago: "These are bright young minds who have been given tremendous responsibility in combat. Thrust them into a conservative bureaucracy and they are going crazy against its illogic."[10] The key challenge remains—how do we encourage our best and brightest to use their experience to help drive innovation in the Navy?

In his departing comments as Chief of Staff of the Air Force General Norton Schwartz noted: "My one regret is that maybe we de-emphasized innovation more than we should have. We had some things to do early on, and we never really came back to pushing that innovative culture."[11]

The Navy Warfare Development Command (NWDC) is taking action on a number of fronts to regain the Navy's innovation advantage. The centerpiece of this effort is an overhaul of the Concept Generation/Concept Development (CGCD) process. The new process streamlines and channels innovative concepts and ideas from the originators to senior leadership. This includes establishing a Chief of Naval Operations (CNO) Advisory Board (CAB) to serve as a lens on the future and champion innovation at the highest levels. Manned by a hybrid mixture of flag officers, scholars, and technology experts, the CAB will look broadly within and beyond the Navy for new warfighting ideas. Its efforts will provide key top-down momentum for innovation. It has worked before and, properly manned and empowered, could work again.

The second development will be a CNO Rapid Innovation Cell (CRIC). This small (and junior) group has established broad connections with industry and small-business innovators to germinate and nurture emerging technologies and concepts. Properly insulated, this "group within a group" could do some amazing things. Author Warren Bennis looked at innovative groups, from Disney to the Manhattan Project, and found "one thing great groups need is protection . . . most traditional organizations say they want innovation, but they reflexively shun the untried."[12] The "free radicals" of the CRIC will be at liberty to move as they see fit while engaging at the front lines of commercial innovation.

The next step for keeping the momentum of new ideas rolling will be a significant effort in experimentation. When aggregated, these broad steps can better focus and help turn new ideas into new capabilities. It has been estimated that for every 3,000 new ideas in business, one survives. A focusing process as described previously can improve our odds.

As the Fleet's center for innovation, NWDC has taken a number of steps to support a "rebirth" of innovation. The Office of Naval Research (ONR) has been a key partner in this effort as the leader in science and technology innovation for the Navy. The collaboration between NWDC and ONR is a good first step. NWDC looks through the lens of the warfighter for ways to mitigate challenges or seize opportunities through the employment of new or existing capabilities. ONR is focused on the creation and development of "leap ahead" technologies. Key points of intersection in these processes include experimentation and rapid fielding. Other key actions taken by NWDC include:

- Resumed funding for tactical development and execution (TAC D&E) projects; a series of smaller efforts to tackle fleet-driven problems.
- In coordination with the ONR, the Naval Postgraduate School, and the Naval War College, NWDC has created a centralized blog site where innovators can propose, debate, and spawn cross-domain ideas. It has turned into a popular "harvesting point" for new thought.
- U.S. Fleet Forces Command has consolidated concept development and Fleet experimentation programs at NWDC, allowing for a synergistic "one-stop" shop for turning new ideas into experiments leading to future capabilities.
- NWDC published the "Innovators Guide," dedicated to helping junior leaders, officers and enlisted, to understand how to push their creative ideas up their chains of command and into development.

In the end, the tomorrow we seek may very well depend on how we harness our creative activities today. Building a streamlined process to drive innovation from the deckplates could be the key. As was so clearly demonstrated during the interwar years, visionary leadership that embraces change as a necessary part of growth, combined with a keen desire to harness the energies of the Fleet, can tailor a future Navy ready to prevail at sea.

## Notes

1. John Kao, *Innovation Manifesto: The Pocket Version for Extremely Busy People* (Hampton Roads, VA: Precision Printing, 2002).
2. John Kao, *Innovation Nation* (New York: Free Press, 2007).
3. Frans Johansson, *The Medici Effect: Breakthrough Insights at the Intersection of Ideas, Concepts & Cultures* (Boston: Harvard Business School Press, 2004), 19.

4.  John T. Kuehn, *Agents of Innovation: The General Board and the Design of the Fleet That Defeated the Japanese* (Annapolis, MD: Naval Institute Press, 2008), 4, 15.

5.  Dr. Donald C. Winter, Secretary of the Navy, speech presented at the Current Strategy Forum, Naval War College, Newport, RI, 13 June 2006.

6.  Term coined by ADM John C. Harvey, Commander USFFC, October 2011.

7.  Kao, *Innovation Nation*.

8.  Speech by ADM John Harvey at NWDC, 13 March 2012.

9.  GEN Martin E. Dempsey, "Mission Command" (Chairman of the Joint Chiefs of Staff White Paper, 3 April 2012).

10. Peter J. Munson, "Disruptive Thinking, Innovation, Whatever You Want to Call It Is Needed for a Military in Crisis," *Small Wars Journal* (blog), 5 April 2012, http://smallwarsjournal.com/blog/disruptive-thinking-innovation-whatever-you-want-to-call-it-is-needed-for-a-military-in-crisis.

11. Interview by Vago Muradian in "This Week in Defense News," 24 July 2012.

12. Warren Bennis, *Organizing Genius: The Secrets of Creative Collaboration* (Cambridge, MA: Perseus Books, 1997), 212.

# 4  "ADAPT, INNOVATE, AND ADAPT SOME MORE"

LtCol Francis G. Hoffman, USMC (Ret.)

**Using three historical case-studies,** Lieutenant Colonel Hoffman seeks to define what the terms "innovation" and "adaptation" mean in the military environment. He cites lessons learned in surface-ship tactics in World War II, antisubmarine action during the Battle of the Atlantic, and unrestricted antisubmarine warfare in the Pacific. Hoffman calls for "a better understanding of the process by which naval organizations have adapted in the past in the competition of combat." He believes the lessons of history can contribute to success in the future.

## "ADAPT, INNOVATE, AND ADAPT SOME MORE"

By LtCol Francis G. Hoffman, USMC (Ret.), U.S. Naval Institute *Proceedings* (March 2014): 30–35.

Three case studies from U.S. naval history emphasize the importance of applying lessons learned in making changes to the way we fight.

The latest conceptual buzzword in U.S. military circles is "adaptation." Drawing on a decade of conflict against asymmetric adversaries, many recognize that the need to learn and adapt does not stop when a war begins. Reinforced by hard-earned lessons from combat over the past decade, innovation must continue on the battlefield. As authors in this journal have emphasized, "adapt or die" is equally true for both evolving species and militaries facing challenging opponents.[1] Those same authors stated: "It is not yet possible to specify exactly what will be involved in institutionalizing rapid adaptability."

Here, we take a step toward specifying what is involved, and use three U.S. Navy case studies to underscore the importance of adaptability in a naval context.

War is an audit of how military institutions and states prepare for war and how their intelligence and force-planning processes succeed in capturing emerging technologies and innovative new methods. It also audits how responsive commanders are to recognize shortfalls or resolve gaps from interaction against a thinking opponent.

The U.S. Army has stressed adaptation for some time. Army theorists have noted: "In the volatile, uncertain, complex and ambiguous environment we face for the foreseeable future, if we were to choose merely one advantage over our adversaries it would certainly be this: to be superior in the art of learning and adaptation."[2] The Army's current capstone concept is based on operational adaptability, calling for "a mindset based on flexibility of thought calling for leaders comfortable with collaborative planning and decentralized execution, a tolerance for ambiguity, and a willingness to make rapid adjustments according to the situation."[3] This definition suggests how adaptability might be exploited, but not created.

The U.S. Navy often gets a bad rap for its unwillingness to change or inability to implement large-scale transformation.[4] President Franklin D. Roosevelt's quip, that trying to change anything in the Navy was like punching into a featherbed, may be apocryphal but not without some validity. Yet operational adaptation is certainly part of U.S. naval history.[5]

## What Is Adaptation?

The military literature is currently undergoing a "surge" in studies on adaptation, with some variation in definitions and implications. Years ago, a book on military innovation, *Military Misfortunes: The Anatomy of Failure in War,* established a framework that covers it in three tenses: future or anticipatory, present tense or adaptive, and post-conflict or learning.[6] "Where learning failures have their roots in the past," Professors Eliot Cohen and John Gooch stress, "adaptive failures suggest an inability to handle the changing present."[7] Also, "The requirement to adapt to unexpected circumstances test both organization and system," they observe, "revealing weaknesses that are partly structural and partly functional."[8] This begs a question about the role institutions have in creating structures and functions (as well as cultures) to support effective learning across all three tenses.

The source of adaptation may vary. Whereas peacetime innovation is usually a deliberate evaluation of options directed by the higher levels of a military, adaptation is arguably generated at the tactical level by results in the battle space, where the relevant information and results are most evident. Recent research, based on field evidence, credibly shows that the direction of innovation during combat is generally from the bottom up; higher headquarters should therefore be flexible to permit organic exploration of new tactics and approaches.[9]

There is a valid question about the scale and character of change required to qualify as innovation or adaptation. Dr. Steve Rosen, in *Winning the Next War,* recognized that innovation could take place either before or during war. He defined innovation either as "a change in one of the primary combat arms of a service in the way it fights" or as creation of a new combat arm.[10] Some define the term as requiring organizational or structural changes and the incorporation of new technologies. Adaptation to others is adjustments to current capabilities and practices, not innovation. A leading scholar, Professor Theo Farrell, defines adaptation as "change to strategy, force generation, and or military plans and operation that is undertaken in response to operational challenges and campaign pressures."[11] This formula emphasizes the source of change, and its institutionalization. The incorporation of adjustments back into Fleet and force generation and training distinguish Dr. Farrell's insights from Dr. John Nagl's *Learning to Eat Soup with a Knife,* where ongoing adjustments against insurgents in Malay were not absorbed into the British Army's doctrine or training.

But, as argued by Cohen and Gooch (and Rosen), innovation can occur before, during, or after a conflict. The scale of innovation can be disruptive or revolutionary, as in an entirely new way of fighting supported by a breakthrough technology, or simply an organizational innovation creating a new capability or set of skills for an institution.

This author accepts Cohen and Gooch's framework. Thus, adaptation emphasizes learning and institutionalizing new skills and competencies. Such competencies may or may not require new organizations or technology, and thus adaptation is a form of military innovation that occurs during wartime in response to interaction with the adversary or unexpected theater conditions. Military adaptation incorporates direct field experience into doctrinal, organizational, and technological solutions to change existing capabilities or create *competencies* that a military organization did not have in its repertoire prior to wartime.

## What Contributes to Adaptation?

Adapting to operational pressures from an opponent requires recognizing a gap and responding in combat. This is the essential question taken on by Colonel Meir Finkel of the Israeli Defense Forces in *On Flexibility*. He notes that military force planners face an increasingly difficult challenge of anticipating or predicting the future battlefield.[12] Rather than focus on predicting the future with precision or overemphasizing intelligence, Finkel studies what contributes to "the ability to recuperate swiftly from the initial surprise." Using historical case studies from World War II to 1973's Yom Kippur War, he examined the rapid implementation of entirely new solutions and technologies forged by the crucible of combat.

His theory builds on what he terms four "strata." The first is conceptual and doctrinal flexibility, the establishment of a climate prepared for all forms of war, accepting the need to challenge official doctrine. The second is organizational and technological diversity, often promoted by emphasizing combined arms and organizational diversity instead of infatuations with wonder weapons and technological fixes. The latter is an area where America's engineering mentality and emphasis on technologically advanced weapons can create problems.

Finkel's third characteristic is flexibility in command and cognitive skills that he attributes to commanders willing to innovate, allowing juniors to challenge precepts or to take the initiative when they find altered conditions. His final stratum incorporates mechanisms for the rapid dissemination of lessons learned in combat so that the entire enterprise benefits. This final element shows how critical communication can be to learning organizations, by broadening the learning accorded adjacent or follow-on units—what might be termed "horizontal dissemination."

Finkel's land-warfare-oriented research is reinforced by Williamson Murray, now at the U.S. Naval War College. In his *Military Adaptation: A Fear of Change*, he concludes: "Over the course of the past century and a half, adaptation in one form or another has been a characteristic of successful military institutions and human societies under the pressures of war." Yet, Murray notes: "Most military organizations and leaders attempt to impose prewar conceptions on the war they are fighting, rather than adapt their assumptions to reality."[13]

Murray's insights suggest the interplay of a realistic appreciation for history and the nature of war, decentralized but competent leadership, rigorous intellectual preparation, and an organizational culture that leans toward critical inquiry and learning new ideas. Regrettably, none of his examples was naval in character. A cross comparison of Finkel's and Murray's attributes is provided below.

Further research is required to determine the correlation between these attributes and successful intra-war adaptation. A few well-recognized Navy historical examples may help, showing how war's audit induced prompt adaptation at sea.

---

### ATTRIBUTES OF ADAPTATION

**FINKEL**
Flexible concepts and doctrine
Organizational and technological diversity
Flexibility in command
Lessons-learned dissemination

**MURRAY**
Realistic doctrine
Mission command
Culture of critical inquiry
Rigorous education

## Naval Case Studies

In August 1942 the U.S. Navy found itself operating in restricted waters protecting the Marine landing on Guadalcanal. The Navy became "immersed in a curriculum of cruel and timeless lessons," in the words of James Hornfischer in *Neptune's Inferno*.[14] A Japanese task force led by Vice Admiral Gunichi Mikawa raced down the Solomon Islands "slot" and evaded detection by destroyer pickets. The Japanese had mastered surface fighting with disciplined training, even tailoring their force and tactics to wear down the anticipated U.S. numerical advantage by emphasizing night operations and the innovative Type 93 Long Lance torpedo.[15]

The action proved short and brutal. In the Battle of Savo Island, 8 August 1942, the Navy lost three heavy cruisers—the USS *Astoria* (CA-34), *Quincy* (CA-71), and *Vincennes* (CA-44)—and two destroyers, as well as the Australian cruiser HMAS *Canberra*. The Japanese escaped relatively unscathed, losing 127 sailors to our 1,077 killed in action. Allied losses were to surface gunfire and Japanese long-range torpedo attack. Comparatively untrained in night fighting and unsure how to best employ their surface-search radar, the U.S. naval task groups suffered devastating losses in the mélée. Admiral Ernest J. King called the results of that single engagement "the blackest day of the whole war," which certainly says something.[16] It probably would have been even worse if Mikawa's force had pressed its attack and gotten to Rear Admiral Richmond Kelly Turner's transports off Guadalcanal. Historian Samuel Eliot Morison was kinder, observing that, "In torpedo tactics and night actions, this series of engagements showed that tactically the Japanese were still a couple of semesters ahead of the United States Navy. . . ."[17]

Well, the U.S. surface force entered night school immediately. Under the direction of Rear Admiral Norman Scott, the cruiser force stepped back, nursed its wounds, and reexamined itself. The forces spent all their free time for the next several weeks in "Night fighting course 101" using the words of one Marine gunner.[18] In short order, the U.S. Navy learned how to successfully conduct surface night actions, improving visual surveillance, integrating both search- and fire-control-radar inputs into the commander's understanding, and improving coordinated maneuver under conditions of both low visibility and chaos. In short, it adapted as a result of its interaction with an enemy who had a coherent night-fighting doctrine and the rigorous training to implement it. The results 90 days later were two much more even battles off Guadalcanal.

## "Not a Battle at All"

Two other examples of U.S. Navy adaptation examine the offensive and defensive dimensions of undersea warfare in World War II. The U.S. Navy was unprepared for battling the U-boat, despite our own and British experiences in World War I. In the 1940s, however, it proved an Allied success. Victory came at a huge cost: between 1939 and 1945, 3,500 Allied merchant ships (14.5 million gross tons) and 175 Allied warships were sunk. More than 117,200 Allied sailors and merchant seamen (mostly British) lost their lives. But the Germans lost 783 U-boats and approximately 30,000 sailors, three-fourths of the country's submarine force.

The Battle of the Atlantic was ultimately the longest campaign in the war, not a battle at all. In tandem with its allies, the U.S. Navy, with support of the Coast Guard and Army Air Forces (post-February 1941), adapted its organization, intelligence, ships, and antisubmarine warfare (ASW) techniques to overcome a determined adversary who also shifted targets, tactics, and technologies. The campaign was eventually won by besting the German Navy in a deadly competition of learning. The relearning of the effectiveness of a comprehensive convoy system proved instrumental, as was fielding adequately equipped destroyer escorts in sufficient numbers. Signals intelligence was invaluable, but so was the continuous evolution of sonar and detection gear, and airborne cover/escorts. The development of improved ASW weapons (depth charges, forward-firing hedgehogs, etc.) also was a major contributor to U-boat attrition.[19]

Adaptation took time, as the U.S. Navy did not want to refight the last war and had forgotten its lessons. The Navy's interwar "genetic encoding" of War Plan Orange, emphasizing carriers and battleships in the Pacific, retarded examination of the ASW challenge.[20] Admiral King's strongly held views on the U.S. Navy's role in the war and the relative priority of Pacific over European requirements may have slowed the development of ASW as a core competency.[21] This lassitude was exacerbated by the need to coordinate externally with the Army Air Forces and to develop ties with the science community. Materiel shortages for escorts and time lags in industrial production also played a role. While Admiral King was personally involved early on, the lack of a dedicated sponsor and organization to prosecute the campaign was not resolved until 10th Fleet stood up, which ironically did not occur until May 1943.[22]

But the Navy did ultimately adapt itself to the challenge, making itself into an effective ASW force. All of Colonel Finkel's factors were evident, especially decentralized approaches and organizational flexibility. Convoy commanders were continually apprised of best practices as they were rapidly gathered and shared, through conferences, reports, and publications.

## Submarines Adapt

The other obvious naval-adaptation case study is founded on our superb submarine operations in the Pacific in World War II. Again prewar innovation, built around two decades of wargaming War Plan Orange, generated an emphasis on carrier air power and amphibious warfare. U.S. planners had a natural moral and cultural resistance to unrestricted warfare and the use of submarines against commercial targets. We also initially lacked an understanding of our adversary's energy dependence and resource vulnerability.

But on 8 December 1941, Admiral Harold Stark ordered the Navy to execute unrestricted warfare against Japan. While not a surprise to the Pacific Fleet's planners, we had neither the commanders nor weapons needed for the task.[23] The submarine community needed to adapt from reconnaissance and screening roles into a true attack force. Fortunately, we had the great advantage of the superior *Gato*-class design. In contrast, we regrettably did not have working torpedoes, proper doctrine, or the personnel and training systems in place to drive the force. The tactics, techniques, and procedures were again developed from the bottom up, backed by leaders who garnered insights from patrol reports, intelligence, the labs of the science community, and operations researchers. Commanders gained tactical insights and trends from their patrol reports, which were distributed both horizontally to others, and vertically up the chain of command.

The force adapted sharply with great effect over time. Japanese shipping losses rose from 134 ships (580,000 tons) in 1942 to 284 ships (1,342,000 tons) in 1943. Once the torpedo problem was fixed by 1944, results doubled again as a total of 492 ships (2,387,000 tons) were sunk or destroyed by submarines. It was a remarkable demonstration of adaptation. Submarines, comprising some 2 percent of the U.S. naval force, were responsible for over half of Japan's maritime losses.[24] Here again, it does not take much imagination to consider how the war in the Pacific might have been altered had the United States begun the war with an offensively oriented submarine force with effective doctrine and operative weapons.

## What Does All This Mean?

These are admittedly short synopses of large and complicated cases. But a few insights can be drawn from them. The Battle of Savo Island is not a major example of innovation, for the U.S. battle fleet already had the required capabilities to counter the Imperial Japanese Navy. The Americans had not ignored night surface attacks.[25] But the Navy certainly had not perfected them to the degree of a competency, and thus some adaptation was required. Better command-and-control practices, improved confidence in using radar, disciplined combat-information-center procedures, and sharper fire-control techniques were all brought to bear. Strong leadership, focused training, some experimentation, and the dissemination of lessons were all contributors.[26]

The other two cases, however, constitute clear-cut adaptations. The U.S. Navy did not develop a new revolutionary way of war, but it learned two naval core competencies the hard way. Success in both theaters was at risk until the Navy mastered ASW in the Atlantic and unrestricted warfare in the Pacific. There are lessons, therefore, in leadership, creating organizations, personnel and leader development, and the close integration of scientific research and/or operations research into combat operations that can be teased out of these case studies. They underscore Colonel Finkel's attributes for flexible command-and-control and lessons-learned dissemination, as well as Professor Murray's emphasis on rigorous education of war and critical inquiry.

Hornfischer's assessment about Guadalcanal is apt about all three cases: "No fighting Navy had ever been so speedily and explosively educated."[27] But we should add that no Navy had ever so rapidly and effectively adapted in two simultaneous and different campaigns in the largest wartime theaters ever seen.

If, as Hoover Institution Senior Fellow Victor Davis Hanson claims, military effectiveness requires an ability to radically change force design or find entirely new competencies, then adaptation could be central to success. Given our inability to predict opponents or the character of future wars, the ability to challenge norms, assumptions, and methods is a fundamental part of success in combat. Chairman of the Joint Chiefs of Staff General Martin Dempsey has properly identified adaptation as a critical lesson over the last decade.[28] In the future, the ability to change rapidly may therefore be a necessity not just a source of relative advantage.

A better understanding of the process by which naval organizations have adapted in the past in the competition of combat should be illuminating. It will shed light on the institutional attributes and culture facilitating critical adaptation. The Navy has mastered this competition in the past, and if history offers any lessons, institutional "adaptivity" will be an enduring contributor to success in future war.[29] This makes it worthy of greater study and understanding.

## Notes

1. Jim Lacey and Kevin Woods, "Adapt or Die," U.S. Naval Institute *Proceedings*, vol. 133, no. 8 (August 2007), 16–21. These authors noted that and that it was a great oversight.
2. David A. Fastabend and Robert H. Simpson, "Adapt or Die: The Imperative for a Culture of Innovation in the United States Army, *Army,* February 2004, 14–25.
3. U.S. Army Training and Doctrine Command, *The Army Capstone Concept—Operational Adaptability: Operating Under Conditions of Uncertainty and Complexity in an Era of Persistent Conflict, 2016–2028* (TRADOC Pam 525–3-0).

4. Peter J. Dombrowski and Andrew L. Ross, "Transforming the Navy: Punching a Featherbed?" *Naval War College Review,* vol. 56, no. 3 (Summer 2003), 107–31.

5. Thomas Mahnken, "Asymmetric Warfare at Sea, The Naval Battles of Guadalcanal, 1942–1943," *Naval War College Review,* vol. 64, no. 1 (Winter 2011), 95–121.

6. Eliot A. Cohen and John Gooch, *Military Misfortunes; The Anatomy of Failure in War* (New York: Free Press, 1996).

7. Ibid., 222.

8. Ibid., 162.

9. James A. Russell, *Innovation, Transformation, and War, Counterinsurgency Operations in Anbar and Ninewa Provinces, Iraq, 2005–2007* (Palo Alto, CA: Stanford Security Studies, 2011).

10. Steven Peter Rosen, *Winning the Next War: Innovation and the Modern Military,* (Ithaca, NY: Cornell University Press, 1991), 7.

11. See Theo Farrell's introduction, "Military Adaptation in War" in Theo Farrell, Frans Osinga, and James A. Russell, eds., *Military Adaptation in the Afghanistan War,* (Palo Alto, CA: Stanford University Press, 2013).

12. Meir Finkel, *On Flexibility, Recovery from Technological and Doctrinal Surprise on the Battlefield* (Palo Alto, CA: Stanford Security Studies, 2011).

13. Williamson Murray, *Military Adaptation: The Fear of Change* (New York: Cambridge University Press, 2012), 3.

14. James D. Hornfischer, *Neptune's Inferno: The U.S. Navy at Guadalcanal* (New York: Random House, 2012), vii.

15. Mahnken, 100–02.

16. Hornfischer, 89.

17. Samuel Eliot Morison, "The Struggle for Guadalcanal, August 1942–February 1943," *The History of United States Naval Operations in World War II,* vol. 5 (Edison, NJ: Castle, 2001), 285.

18. Hornfischer, 137–39. The quote is at 137.

19. See Clay Blair, *Hitler's U-Boat War: The Hunted, 1942–1945* (New York: Random House/Modern Library, 2000), which is indispensable to understanding the "tonnage" war of attrition played by both sides.

20. See Michael Vlahos, *The Blue Sword: The Naval War College and the American Mission, 1919–1941* (Newport, RI: Naval War College Press, 1980).

21. See Montgomery C. Meigs, *Slide Rules and Submarines* (Washington, DC: National Defense University Press, 1990), xxii, 218.

22. Samuel Eliot Morison, "The Battle of the Atlantic: September 1939–May 1943," vol. 1, *The History of the U.S. Naval Operations in World War II* (Annapolis, MD: Naval Institute Press, 2010).

23. Joel Ira Holwitt, *"Execute Against Japan," The U.S. Decision to Conduct Unrestricted Submarine Warfare* (College Station, TX: Texas A&M University Press, 2009). See James F. DeRose, *Unrestricted Warfare; How a New Breed of Officers Led the Submarine Force to Victory in World War II* (Edison, NJ: Castle Books, 2006).

24. Clay Blair, *Silent Victory: The U.S. Submarine War Against, Japan,* vol. 2 (New York: Lippincott, 1975), 853.

25. Trent Hone, "'Give Them Hell!' The U.S. Navy's Night Combat Doctrine and the Campaign for Guadalcanal," *War in History* vol. 13, no. 2 (April 2006), 171–99.

26. On Scott's fleetwide bulletins, see Hornfischer, 139.

27. Ibid., vii.

28. LGEN George Flynn, USMC, "A Decade at War" (Suffolk, VA: Joint Chiefs of Staff, June 2012).

29. See Anne-Marie Grisogono and Vanja Radenovic, "The Adaptive Stance" (Fairbairn, Canberra, Australia: Defence Science and Technology Organisation, 2006).

# 5 "PAYLOADS OVER PLATFORMS: CHARTING A NEW COURSE"

ADM Jonathan W. Greenert, USN

In this article, the Chief of Naval Operations addresses the need to prioritize *payloads* over *platforms*, because operational flexibility and adaptation will be critical to keeping a given platform relevant over a lifetime that could extend up to fifty years. Greenert cites the Littoral Combat Ship (LCS) as an example of a flexible platform that can be configured to carry varied sensors, weapons, and mission packages, thus maximizing its ability to change to meet emerging threats. He declares that "decoupling the development of payloads from the development of platforms is an imperative for us to take advantage of the fundamental trends shaping our operating environment."

## "PAYLOADS OVER PLATFORMS: CHARTING A NEW COURSE"

By ADM Jonathan W. Greenert, USN, U.S. Naval Institute *Proceedings* (July 2012): 16–23.

Navy platforms, particularly ships and aircraft, are large capital investments frequently designed to last for 20 to 50 years. To ensure our Navy stays relevant, these platforms have to adapt to the changing fiscal, security, and technological conditions they will encounter over their long service lives. It is unaffordable, however, to adapt a platform by replacing either it or its integral systems each time a new mission or need arises. We will instead need to change the modular weapon, sensor, and unmanned vehicle "payloads" a platform carries or employs. In addition to being more affordable, this decoupling of payload development from platform development will take advantage of a set of emerging trends in precision weapons, stealth, ship and aircraft construction, economics, and warfare I will describe in this article.

One example of a payload-centric approach to adaptability is the USS *Enterprise* (CVN-65), which celebrated her 50th birthday last year. The *Enterprise* was conceived in the 1950s to deal with a growing Soviet threat. At the time our national strategy was to contain the Soviet Union, which required aircraft carriers that could quickly reposition and project power on the Soviet periphery, thereby avoiding its sizable garrisons of ground forces and land-based aircraft. A large, nuclear-powered aircraft carrier with specialized fighters and attack aircraft provided a solution to these operational requirements.

## Why Modular Makes Sense

The evolution of the *Enterprise*'s concept of operations and systems over the past five decades offers an important insight for future ship and aircraft development. Substantial volume, reserve electrical power, and a small number of integral warfare systems were needed to address the warfighting requirements of the *Enterprise*. Those characteristics coincidently made it easier to adapt the *Enterprise*'s capability over time. In contrast, most of today's ships and aircraft were designed in the latter days of the Cold War, with limited reserve capacity and integral systems of sensors, processors, and weapons for the entire range of high-end missions against the Soviets: antisubmarine warfare (ASW), integrated air and missile defense (IAMD), antiair warfare (AAW), surface warfare (SUW), and strike. Although those complex platforms (and our superb sailors) have adapted to new missions over the past 20-plus years, most of our ships and aircraft remain fully loaded "luxury sedans," taking their full multimission kit with them wherever they go through their whole service lives.

Navy missions since the Cold War evolved to include defeating terrorists, pirates, and illegal traffickers; preparing to counter mines and armed small boats; providing humanitarian assistance/disaster relief; and building partnership capacity to take on maritime-security missions. Those operations show one limitation of a highly integrated luxury-car platform. While the ship, aircraft, and crew might flex to new or different missions, it does so at a cost. Destroyer crews are challenged to maintain proficiency in core missions such as ASW, SUW, and IAMD when engaged in months-long counterpiracy operations. Amphibious ships are in high demand for counterterrorism and humanitarian-assistance operations and have had limited opportunity to practice amphibious assault. And P-3C crews had their ASW capabilities atrophy after a decade of high-tempo intelligence, surveillance, and reconnaissance operations over land.

To more efficiently match platform to mission in the future we will need to treat capabilities as being inherent in the payloads a platform carries and employs, rather than capabilities being inherent (integrated) in the platform itself. In *Sailing Directions* and *Navigation Plan for 2013,* I highlighted my intent to "expand the reach and effectiveness of ships and aircraft through new payloads of weapons, unmanned systems and sensors." The use of modular payloads that can be changed out over a platform's life offers an effective and affordable way to maintain our adaptability and warfighting advantage against evolving threats.

## The Precision-Weapons Revolution

The predominant trend compelling us to consider a new approach for capability development is the exponential growth of information-processing power. Over the past 40 years, that growth helped fuel innovation in almost every civilian and military technology, and brought about a revolution in the precision and accuracy of sensors and weapons. In 1965, Gordon Moore, co-founder of Intel, predicted that the number of transistors per processor chip would double about every two years, thereby increasing overall computing speed and power. His prediction—now commonly referred to as "Moore's Law"—held true. Today's commercially available chips are almost 40,000 times faster than those available in 1971.[1] Moreover, the average price of a megabyte of computer memory has gone from more than $700,000 dollars in 1970 to around 2 cents today.[2]

The precision weapons enabled by this computing power fundamentally changed modern warfare. Advances in targeting and guidance systems allow us to achieve much greater accuracy and lethality with far fewer weapons. Today, about 70–80 percent of guided munitions fall within ten yards of their targets. During World War II only 18 percent of U.S. bombs fell within 1,000 feet of their targets.[3]

Our commanders exploit this precision by using the smallest number and size of weapons possible. In addition to improving efficiency, this minimizes collateral damage—which can have a significant strategic impact in modern counterinsurgency operations. From World War II to the Gulf War, the number of bombs used to hit a fixed target decreased by a factor of 300, the number of aircraft assigned decreased by a factor of almost 400, and bombing accuracy improved by a factor of 17.[4] Instead of sorties per aimpoint, we now commonly speak in terms of aimpoints per sortie.

The ability of a few very precise standoff weapons to be more efficient and effective than a larger number of less-precise weapons leads to a surprising result. In modern warfare, precision standoff weapons such as Tomahawk or the joint standoff weapon are now more cost-effective in many situations than short-range gravity bombs such as the joint direct attack munition (JDAM). A Tomahawk missile, for example, costs about $1.2 million, while a JDAM is about $30,000. To strike a single target, however, the total training, maintenance, and operations cost to get a manned aircraft close enough to deliver the JDAM is several times higher than the cost of launching 3 Tomahawk at the same target from a destroyer, submarine or aircraft operating several hundred miles away. That is one of the trends leading us to focus more effort on improving and evolving our standoff sensor and munition payloads.

## The Limits of Stealth

The rapid expansion of computing power also ushers in new sensors and methods that will make stealth and its advantages increasingly difficult to maintain above and below the water. First, though, military sensors will start to circumvent stealth of surface ships and aircraft through two main mechanisms:

- Operating at lower electromagnetic frequencies than stealth technologies are designed to negate, and
- Detecting the stealth platform from angles or aspects at which the platform has a higher signature.

U.S. forces can take advantage of those developments by employing long-range sensor, weapon, and unmanned-vehicle payloads instead of using only stealth platforms and shorter-range systems to reach targets.

Stealth ships and aircraft are designed to have a small radar or infrared electromagnetic signature at specific frequencies. The frequency ranges at which stealth is designed to be most effective are those most commonly used by active radar or passive infrared detection systems. At lower frequencies detections do not normally provide the resolution or precision necessary for accurate targeting. Using more powerful information-processing, however, military forces will be able to develop target-quality data from these lower-frequency passive infrared signals or active-radar returns.[5]

The aspects at which stealth platforms are designed to have their smallest signature are those from which detection is most likely. For example, an aircraft or ship is designed to have a small signature or radar return when it is approaching a threat sensor—or has a "nose-on" aspect. Improved computer processing will produce new techniques that can detect stealth platforms at target aspects from which they have higher radar returns. Multiple active radars, for instance, can combine their returns through a battle-management computer so radar detections from a stealth platform's less-stealthy side, underside, or rear aspect can be shared and correlated to allow the stealth platform to be detected and attacked. Similarly, passive radar receivers can capture the electromagnetic energy that comes from transmitters of opportunity—such as cellphone or TV towers—and bounces off a stealth platform at a variety of angles. With better processing in the future, those weak, fragmented signals can be combined to create actionable target information.[6]

Those developments do not herald the end of stealth, but they do show the limits of stealth design in getting platforms close enough to use short-range weapons. Maintaining stealth in the face of new and diverse counter-detection methods would require significantly higher fiscal investments in our next generation of platforms. It is time to consider shifting our focus from platforms that rely solely on stealth to also include concepts for operating farther from adversaries using standoff weapons and unmanned systems—or employing electronic-warfare payloads to confuse or jam threat sensors rather than trying to hide from them.

## Faster Refresh, Exploiting the Learning Curve

The average time required to research, develop, and construct a new U.S. ship or aircraft is now more than 15 years, or about eight cycles of Moore's Law. For example, the *Arleigh Burke*–class destroyer took 14 years from initial requirement to the lead ship's commissioning. That by itself is not necessarily a problem. Most of our ship and aircraft classes will be in service for decades. We should retain a deliberate, comprehensive, and effective process to design them from scratch.

Meanwhile, rapidly improving information-processing has sped up the technology "refresh" cycle. Consumer electronics are completing a generation every one to two years, and we tapped into that faster innovation cycle over the past decade with some of our off-the-shelf technology insertion efforts in surface-ship and submarine combat systems. Those initiatives, however, work at the "payload" scale, rather than on a whole platform.

Payloads offer a more rapid means to improve or integrate new capabilities into a proven platform. In contrast to the 15 to 20 years to design and deliver a new ship or aircraft, a prototype or demonstration weapon, sensor, or unmanned-vehicle payload has been developed, assembled, and installed on an existing platform in as little as a few months. In Bahrain, we are outfitting our patrol coastal ships with Mk-38 gyro-stabilized guns and Griffin antiship missiles within nine months of the decision to upgrade; in the Mediterranean, we integrated the Fire Scout unmanned air vehicle on frigates and used it for surveillance during Operation Unified Protector in Libya; and in the Middle East, within six months of identifying a need, we outfitted our deploying helicopters with upgraded Mk-54 torpedoes.

Payloads also offer a more cost-effective way to integrate capability into today's platforms. The cost of ships and aircraft has risen by as much as 500 percent (in constant dollars) since the mid-1960s. Much of that increase is due to the inherent complex capabilities built into our platforms, not the hull or airframe itself. But once the requirements for a new ship or aircraft are locked down and the ship goes into production, the builders' learning curve enables each successive hull or airframe to be built for less cost than its predecessor. Some recent examples of this are the *Virginia*-class submarines, for which the builder reduced the number of construction man-hours by 30 percent from the first hull to the most recent, or *Arleigh Burke*–class destroyers, where cost dropped by more than 20 percent between the first and second flight. Keeping a proven hull or airframe in serial production for as long as possible gives us the largest (and longest) return on our research-and-development investment.

Taking advantage of that learning curve while ensuring each hull or airframe has relevant capability for its time requires that we look at platforms more as trucks. The truck will load and plug in successive generations of modular payloads as it goes through decades of serial production. To support that approach, we would increasingly employ standardized interfaces to plug in new sensors, weapons, and unmanned systems; and standardized links to communicate with them if they leave the truck. The design of future platforms also must take into account up front the volume, electrical power, cooling, speed, and survivability needed to effectively incorporate new payloads throughout their service lives.

## First Steps

Focusing on payloads is not a completely new idea, and the Navy has pursued payload-centric capability development in the past. In most cases, however, those projects adapted a purpose-built platform, as opposed to designing a ship or aircraft from the keel up to host changing payloads. In 1994, for example, the concept of a stealthy arsenal ship loaded with large numbers of land-attack cruise missiles was proposed, but after two years of analysis it was deemed unaffordable and terminated. About the same time, as a result of the 1994 Nuclear Posture Review the Navy removed four *Ohio*-class SSBNs from service. Seeing an opportunity to continue using those ships, in 2002 the Navy began converting them into guided-missile submarines—SSGNs. The adaptation allowed the SSGNs to carry new payloads of missiles (up to 154 Tomahawk land-attack cruise missiles, or TLAM) and special operations forces (SOF), effectively becoming an arsenal ship.

Today we are planning to replace the SSGNs' TLAM capacity when they retire with the *Virginia* payload module (VPM), integrated into *Virginia*-class SSNs already in serial production. VPMs will be designed to host a variety of payloads beyond TLAM to include large-displacement unmanned underwater vehicles and SOF operators and their systems. VPMs will more than triple the missile capacity of our current *Virginia*-class SSNs (from 12 to 40 TLAMs) and provide access from inside the submarine to service VPM payloads.

We also have taken a payload-centric approach in some aspects of surface-ship design. Armored box launchers for Tomahawk missiles were fielded in the early 1980s on battleships and nuclear-powered cruisers. This system evolved into the Mk-41 vertical launching system (VLS) introduced on *Ticonderoga*-class cruisers in 1986 and retrofitted on some *Spruance*-class destroyers. VLS is a modularized below-deck launcher with standard cell sizes and standard interfaces for power, cooling, and computing. This standardization allowed rapid integration of new weapon payloads over the ships' life. Aboard cruisers, VLS payload options expanded from TLAM in 1986 to now include the standard missile family (SM-2, SM-3, and SM-6) and ASW rockets (ASROC). VLS is the main battery of *Arleigh Burke*–class destroyers, and in addition to SM-family missiles and ASROC now includes the Evolved Sea Sparrow Missile for short-range air defense. Today, 8,372 VLS cells are deployed in the U.S. surface fleet, each of which can hold a growing range of payloads. VLS is also deployed in 11 allied navies, providing opportunities to "pool" weapons and other payloads in Europe or East Asia for all VLS users. This is a cost-effective model to integrate new payloads aboard proven platforms and well worth the upfront investment in ship power, cooling, and standard interfaces.

We also are in the early stages of incorporating unmanned payloads on our manned ships to further expand their reach on, above, and below the sea. Starting in 2005, we began equipping amphibious ships (LPDs, LSDs, and LHAs) and destroyers with the Scan Eagle UAV under a services contract for maritime and littoral intelligence, surveillance, and reconnaissance (ISR). Operating for up to 15 hours at a nominal range of 50 nautical miles from its host platform, Scan Eagle provides critical and unobtrusive day and night imagery in support of counterterrorism, counterpiracy, surface warfare, and irregular warfare missions—as well as helping to uncover other illicit activities at sea.

The MQ-8B Fire Scout vertical take-off UAV debuted in 2009 aboard frigates to support a range of ISR missions, including service in Operation Unified Protector in Libya and in support of counterpiracy operations around Africa. We will introduce an improved MQ-8C (Fire—X) UAV next year that uses a helicopter airframe with greater range and capacity—allowing it to conduct surveillance and strike missions in support of special-operations forces. The control systems for Scan Eagle and Fire Scout can be removed and reinstalled in a relatively short time for deployment, making them an effective way to rapidly change the capability of the host platform.

Aircraft naturally lend themselves to a payload focus, because they are designed with hard points and junctions into which a number of modular payloads can be connected. The F/A-18 Hornet, for example, can carry a wide range of weapons or sensors, from antiship Harpoon missiles and targeting pods to antiair advanced medium range air-to-air missiles. Similarly, the P-8A Poseidon maritime patrol aircraft will be able to carry torpedoes, Harpoon missiles, bombs, and sonobuoys that can evolve over time to address changing threats or incorporate new technologies.

Those examples are certainly moving us in the right direction. We will continue to work to decouple payload development from platform development and design platforms from the start to accommodate a changing portfolio of payloads. This will allow us to build the same hulls and airframes for decades and exploit the industrial learning curve while still evolving our capabilities to keep our warfighting edge against improving adversaries. In particular, we need longer-range weapons to allow platforms to reach our foes despite their improvements in sensors. We need more capable and more numerous electronic-warfare and cyber payloads to thwart detection and targeting. We need unmanned payloads that expand the reach of today's platforms both for sensing and attack. And we need volume in our platforms to accommodate the people and equipment for new missions.

## Moving Forward

Our first "keel up" application of a payload focus is the littoral combat ship (LCS). The heart of the LCS's payload flexibility is its interface-control document (ICD). That ICD specifies how payloads plug into ship computer networks, power, and cooling, and describes the space available to host new payloads and operators. Similar to the USB port on today's personal computers, the ICD provides a common reference for payload developers seeking to design mission packages for an LCS. We are currently developing surface warfare, mine warfare, and antisubmarine warfare mission packages for the LCS. With the ICD, the payloads within these mission packages can evolve over time to take advantage of new technologies or to address new threats.

We plan to send the *Freedom* (LCS-1) to Singapore early next year to evaluate the LCS operational concept, including the SUW mission package, in a relevant operational environment. The adaptability of the LCS to new payloads allows us to adjust the systems in the mission package based on the lessons learned from this deployment and future operations. We will need to be disciplined in modifying payloads, however, to avoid introducing new cost increases through too-frequent modifications.

We will use reserve capacity and standardized interfaces to introduce a range of payloads in new platforms such as the mobile landing platform (two of which will be built to serve as an afloat forward staging base), joint high-speed vessel, and P-8A. We will also look to employ a changing set of payloads on our existing amphibious ships, destroyers, aircraft carriers, and submarines.

## Affordably Keeping Our Warfighting Edge

Decoupling the development of payloads from the development of platforms is an imperative for us to take advantage of the fundamental trends shaping our operating environment. Technology, especially information-processing, will continue to evolve more quickly and become more widely available, while new ship and aircraft classes likely will continue to require more than a decade to join the Fleet. We appear to be reaching the limits of how much a platform's inherent stealth can affordably get it close enough to survey or attack adversaries. And our fiscal situation will continue to require difficult trade-offs, requiring us to look for new ways to control costs while remaining relevant.

Common hulls and airframes will decrease and stabilize shipbuilding and aircraft construction costs through the learning curve of serial production. At the same time, shifting to modular payloads as the primary source of capability enables us to more rapidly and affordably incorporate new technology. Just as Apple's fleet of platforms has provided incentives for the development of new "apps" and peripheral devices that easily plug into its operating system, the Navy can spur the development of new capabilities and payloads to plug into the Fleet. This model will help us to maintain our warfighting edge, build the Fleet capacity that keeps us forward, and improve our readiness for today's missions. We will work together with our industry partners to put this concept into action, so our Navy can continue to sustainably protect our nation's security and prosperity.

## Notes

1. See download.intel.com/pressroom/kits/IntelProcessorHistory.pdf.

2. See www.jcmit.com/memoryprice.htm and Dave Bursky, "Nonvolatile Memory Cuts the Price of Digital Storage," *Electronic Design,* 21 January 2002, 25.

3. Robert A. Pape, "The True Worth of Air Power," *Foreign Affairs,* 83.2 (2004) 116.

4. Richard P. Hellion, *Storm Over Iraq* (Washington, DC: Smithsonian Press, 1992) 190. See also Paul G. Gillespie, *Weapons of Choice: The Development of Precision Guided Munitions* (Tuscaloosa: University of Alabama, 2006).

5. Bill Sweetman, "Stealth Threat," *Popular Science,* December 2001, www .popsci.com/military-aviation-space/article/2001–12/stealth-threat. See also Arend G. Westra, "Radar versus Stealth," *Joint Forces Quarterly,* 55 (2009) 136–143.

6. Bill Sweetman, "Stealth Threat," *Popular Science,* December 2001, www .popsci.com/military-aviation-space/article/2001–12/stealth-threat. See also Arend G. Westra, "Radar versus Stealth," *Joint Forces Quarterly,* 55 (2009) 136–143.

# 6 "MAKING ROOM FOR RISK: MANAGING DISRUPTIVE TECHNOLOGIES"

RADM James Stavridis, USN

We opened this section with an excerpt from the book Admiral Stavridis wrote from his perspective as a recently retired four-star admiral. We close the section by presenting what then–rear admiral Stavridis had to say about dealing with disruptive technologies from his earlier vantage-point as a Navy two-star. Although it is not the subject of this article, it is interesting to note that he wrote this article just weeks prior to the incredibly disruptive attacks of 9/11. The technology (commercial airliners) employed by the terrorists was hardly new, but it was used to devastating and horrific effect.

## "MAKING ROOM FOR RISK: MANAGING DISRUPTIVE TECHNOLOGIES"

By RADM James Stavridis, USN, U.S. Naval Institute *Proceedings* (September 2001): 32–36.

We are awash in a sea of disruptive technology. Each day, it seems, there are dramatic emergent advances trumpeted in various industries: new generation computer chips, smaller communicative and connective devices, genetic enhancements, bioengineering marvels, indestructible polymers and veneers—at times one feels as though tomorrow arrives here newly minted every hour.

The hard part is that most, if not all, of these technologies threaten to disrupt existing products and markets, producing turmoil and requiring difficult decisions by managers and planners across a variety of industries—including the military. Yet, they offer ultimately enormous rewards in terms of what they can deliver. How can we leverage the inherent goodness in such disruptive technologies in a way that maximizes benefits and minimizes confusion and failure?

This is, of course, hardly a new problem. The emergence of such new technologies—which are potentially threatening to embedded legacy systems and procedural norms—is as old as the notion of business cycles itself. In the military context, we have dealt with this in the endless cycle of shifting predominance between offense and defense in combat—from heavily armored ships to bigger caliber guns at sea in the early part of this century, for example. But today, the *pace* of emergence of disruptive technologies threatens to swamp the military's ability to incorporate and use such advancements. Managing such disruptive technologies is a vast and fundamental early 21st-century challenge.

Another way to say this is that we are reasonably capable of inventing and discovering disruptive technology—the military "has funded the pre-award research of 58 percent of the nation's Nobel prize winners in chemistry and 43 percent of laureates in physics"[1]—but not so effective in managing its incorporation. Overall, it appears that business is recognizing and grappling with the management of disruptive technology well ahead of the military. As a result, there are lessons to be learned both from an examination of business case experience and from how the business world is coping.

## In Business: Changing How We Communicate, Compute, Copy

Disruptive technologies in the business sense "create major new growth in the industries they penetrate—even when they cause traditionally entrenched firms to fail—by allowing less-skilled and less-affluent people to do things previously done only by expensive specialists in centralized, inconvenient locations."[2] In the simplest sense, disruptive technologies are things that improve on a current product but initially seem too expensive and too limited in capability to make business sense, which leads businesses to "hold on to the old" rather than move to embrace the new technologies.

A couple of examples will help clarify the idea. Reaching back, an early 20th-century example is the telephone, which threatened to disrupt the well-established telegraph. Initially, telephones could carry a signal only a few miles, and Western Union therefore rejected the idea of pursuing commercial development of the telephone because it could not match the long-distance capability of the embedded telegraph system. "The Bell telephone therefore took root as a local communications service that was simple enough to be used by everyday people. Little by little, the telephone's range improved until it supplanted Western Union and its telegraph operators altogether."[3]

Another classic disruptive technology is the personal computer. When PCs first appeared on the market, they were no challenge to mainframe computers in power or usefulness. Apple and Atari marketed the first ones, essentially as toys. Many mainframe makers, and even minicomputer manufacturers, missed the emergence of the smaller PCs, preferring to cling to their larger and more powerful legacy systems long after market indicators forecast the leap to the PC.

In the photocopier marketplace, Xerox initially dominated with large, powerful, centralized copiers; yet companies such as Ricoh and Canon gradually have introduced small, inexpensive copiers—essentially disruptive technologies—and dramatically improved their market shares. Other examples abound, from the development of the small, personal camera by George Eastman, which disrupted the market for large, stationary, box cameras, to the introduction of the DVD player, which is disrupting the lucrative VCR market today. Most analysts believe this accelerating trend of disruption increasingly will define the business cycle.[4]

Business has gotten better at dealing with such disruptive technologies over the past several decades, but in the military we are not improving as quickly. Representative Mac Thornberry (R-TX), a leading voice on defense reform, outlines the comparison: "Ford can take a car from concept to customer in less than 24 months, Compaq can change its computer manufacturing requirements in 1 day, and Boeing can develop and field a 777 in less than 5 years. Yet under today's procurement rules, it now takes more than a decade to field a military system. The F-22 is still in development 18 years after it was begun."[5] We can do better. We must do better.

## In the Military: Racing to Apply Technology

In the military context, the cycle of emergent disruptive technology is equally evident. In the early 20th century, primitive radios were developed to communicate between warships at sea. They were bulky, expensive, and prone to failure—and they were rejected in favor of continued use of visual signals. Yet, eventually the benefits became so evident that, after much delay and rejection, the new technology penetrated the fleet.

The classic mid-20th-century naval example is the development of attack carrier air power at sea. The battleships' "big gun club" fought what might have been the longest and most public rear-guard action in the history of military technology, and managed to delay full-out development and production of carrier air for decades.

More recent examples, some still playing out, are cruise missiles, which challenge manned tactical aviation; stealth configurations of maritime and aviation platforms, which challenge more conventional structures; and network-centric warfare, which challenges traditional methods of strike and command and control.

Looking to the future, there are several coming disruptive technologies in the naval "business." Unmanned vehicles, in both the air and the sea, increasingly will challenge manned aircraft, ships, and submarines. Indeed, the same pattern of utilization observed in the introduction of manned aircraft at sea—first for scouting, then distant communication, and eventually, attack—is being replayed in the unmanned vehicle and combat aerial vehicle debate. The Air Force, for example, is looking increasingly at placing weapons and advanced sensor packages on its Predator unmanned aerial vehicle.

Also on the horizon is electric-drive propulsion, which challenges conventional drive solutions for large warships. Planned for incorporation in the Navy's

DD-21, electric drive promises eventually to be quieter, cheaper, and more flexible in its distribution of power in ships—but it will have to prove itself in a potentially drawn-out period while older, established gas turbine and steam systems continue to hold center stage.

Information attack systems also are emerging as disruptive technologies with importance to all aspects of potential combat operations. While not technically well understood today, expensive to develop, and subject to significant policy criticism, information attack technologies eventually could challenge a wide variety of alternative means of attack, particularly hard-kill options.

Other, perhaps more distant, disruptive technologies might include biological systems, from performance-enhancing drugs to man-machine interfaces; miniaturization at all levels, to include tiny killer-sensor devices; new polymers and compounds that provide enhanced defensive options; laser and other directed-energy weapons; sensors that optically or thermally penetrate mid-to-deep ocean areas; and hyperefficient fuel cells and microturbines.

There are many others. One recent study mentions, for example, technologies "for distributed, micro-satellite constellations; space-based radars with moving target indicator capabilities; unmanned systems, to include micro-robots and micro-UAVs; performance-enhancing exoskeletons; next-generation stealth, including applications to air mobility aircraft, surface naval vessels and ground combat systems; hypersonic and directed-energy systems; and micro-proximity satellites for space control."[6]

Clearly there is no shortage of candidates; the real challenge is winnowing and harvesting—in a word, managing—such potentially disruptive technologies.

## Investing for the Long Sail

How can the military in general—and the sea services in particular—best position itself to take advantage of disruptive technologies? Essentially, we must establish mechanisms, as business has, to embrace creative disruptive technologies in ways that do not place national security at risk or prematurely discard still vital and useful older systems. At the same time, we must ensure that potential opponents are not able to leverage our research-and-development efforts to "coast," skimming the benefits of our expensive revolution in a cheaper "second revolution."

On "our side" of the issue, several general tenets will help us manage disruptive technology effectively:

- *Be open to ideas and protective of those who advocate disruptive technologies.* We need to work hard to widen the aperture of what is "permitted" in terms of discussion. This applies across the board, from the smallest conferences of mid-grade officers debating programmatic options to the most senior discussions of the sea service leadership, to include resource sponsors and requirements assessors on the Navy, Marine Corps, and Coast Guard staffs. As part of this spirit of openness, we must encourage the mavericks in practical terms—calling attention on fitness reports to innovation, for example. We should consider a "year out" program to send officers into the private sector in lieu of a fellowship or war college—and recognize this in a career perspective as the equivalent of a master's degree.

- *Examine how businesses develop and integrate disruptive technologies over the longer term.* We should learn how major businesses are doing this in ways that look beyond the immediately practical to decide what to invest in for the long term. We should explore what the Central Intelligence Agency has done with In-Q-Tel, which merges public and private solutions in an acquisition sense (see sidebar, below). We also should look for and encourage micro-economic development units, fondly known as the "bicycle shops." This is where the mantra of "skip a generation" may actually play out. While the services do this to some extent with their Tactical Exploitation of National Capabilities (TENCap) programs, clearly this is an area of potential expansion in the context of finding, nurturing, and introducing disruptive technologies.

- *Get strategy and money talking together.* This does not happen naturally, as organizations chartered with strategic long-range planning and technological long-range planning are split as separate entities. Business does

## IN-Q-TEL: BRINGING NEXT-GENERATION TECHNOLOGIES TO THE CIA

Founded in 1999, In-Q-Tel is an independent, private, nonprofit company chartered by the Central Intelligence Agency (CIA) with one objective: to identify and deliver the next generation of information technologies to support the CIA's critical intelligence missions. As the agency's "venture catalyst," In-Q-Tel partners with leading innovators to catalyze technologies, bring them quickly to market, and at the same time bring them to bear on the CIA's most pressing IT problems.

In-Q-Tel's CEO and president, Gilman Louie, explains, "Congress and the CIA, under the leadership of George Tenet, recognized that the CIA needed a new way to tackle its critical technology needs. The agency saw that the people who are leading innovation are all around us. They are the entrepreneurs of the knowledge economy. They are the private-sector investors putting billions into information technology development. The CIA's idea was to combine its own talent with these private-sector resources—to put them together to help solve the real problems the agency faces today. In-Q-Tel was created as part of a broader effort initiated by the agency to get ahead of its IT needs."

To do that, In-Q-Tel works with private and public companies in the United States and abroad, as well as with universities, established companies, and national and private labs. A hybrid of public- and private-sector models, In-Q-Tel has the flexibility to structure relationships using whatever approaches work best, including equity investments, development project funding, and spin-offs. In-Q-Tel's strategy is to target technologies that provide commercial analogs to the CIA's IT problems. It focuses on such technologies as Internet search and discovery, information security and privacy, enterprise knowledge management, and geospatial applications.

"We've had some early success," notes Louie. "In 18 months of operations, we've engaged more than 800 companies, three-quarters of which had never done business with the government before. We also have built a network of more than 60 different venture funds that have laid out their portfolios of companies asking to engage us in a dialogue of value. We've partnered with more than 15 companies so far, and we've delivered five technologies into the CIA. It's a good start, but we know there is a lot of work ahead to achieve a real strategic difference for the agency."

this far better than we do, and many corporations are creating specifically chartered "idea factories" to merge strategy and technology at the highest corporate levels.

On our opponents' side of the issue, we need to develop mechanisms to protect our sunk costs in research and development from providing direct and rapid benefit to our opponents. Security regimes must be carefully implemented and our prototypes well controlled. In addition, we should consider creating "false trails" to take potential opponents down technological blind alleys. Finally, we need to "red team" our own disruptive technology systems to understand their vulnerability to reverse engineering and low-cost exploitation.

Beyond these general points, a cluster of specific ideas seems worth pursuing:

- *Create an idea factory on the sea service staffs.* We should consider having this as a direct report at a senior level, populated by a small group of creative and innovative technologists and strategists. Let them identify a series of small, specific disruptive technologies to challenge the orthodoxy. We have thousands of staff officers working on the conventional ideas; let's put some resources against the unconventional. These idea factories should be the places strategy, technology, and money meet; they need access to the full range of current and future plans.
- *Be prepared to conduct rigorous and unbiased analysis.* Take the ideas from the "factory" and put them through the ringer. As part of this, we should consider approaching the Department of Defense with the idea of implementing a two-year defense budget—and possibly multiyear commitments to specific technology explorations—for research and development, to allow longer time lines for our analytic efforts.[7] There is plenty of room in this step (and in the previous one) for input and interaction from organizations such as the Office of Naval Research, Defense Advanced Research Projects Agency, Naval Warfare Development Center, and Strategic Studies Group.
- *Build a cadre of innovators.* We need people with both pure intellectual firepower and a creative turn of mind and who are capable of fusing

two disparate disciplines: strategy and technology. Perhaps we should consider building a new curriculum at the Naval Postgraduate School or the Naval War College. In addition, early 20th-century innovators such as Sims, Moffett, and Mitchell all had longevity—albeit they had enemies and had to fight for position. As Andy Marshall (an innovator with a good deal of longevity himself) has pointed out, "Moffett was appointed three times to a five year term. Today, even if you had a great guy in a key position, he would disappear in two years."[8] Each of the services has created and protected a corps of acquisition experts—AP, or acquisition professional, in Navy parlance—a good step. Now we should consider how to create and protect innovators.

- *Emphasize prototyping and leasing.* One key problem with the culture of experimentation is deciding when to buy, and then when to produce en masse. We need an approach that allows cost-effective leasing of commercial possibilities and prototyping of systems we want to try out that are not being produced commercially. As the recent U.S. Commission on National Security commented, "Prototyping of weapons systems, which allows the possibility that some attempts will fail, and then developing and producing the most promising concepts, will get the 'kinks' out of systems early and shorten development cycle time."[9] It also will promote acceptance of disruptive technologies and ultimately useful systems. We may be able to expand service TENCap and joint advanced concept technology demonstration programs in this regard.

- *Explore a "dual track" procurement system.* Put major programs on a traditional path, but allow a second, accelerated path for a small number of systems that are potentially disruptive—and therefore "threatening"—to the major systems. Such disruptive systems would be of particular use in cutting-edge technologies such as information operations, communications, and biologics. While this is in the realm of Congress and the Secretary of Defense's office, the services could consider proposing this idea.

- *Continue to explore business lessons.* Dr. Clayton Christensen, a leading authority on these issues and professor at Harvard Business School, lists five basic tenets from the business perspective, each of which can be applied on the military side: (1) Give responsibility for disruptive technologies to organizations whose customers need them; (2) set up a separate organization dedicated to developing these technologies; (3) expect some initiatives will fail and be prepared to terminate them and try something else; (4) don't count on sudden breakthroughs; and (5) recognize at the beginning, the new technologies will not be attractive to sophisticated high-end users. There are lessons in the U.S. business community on dealing with disruptive technology. We should reach out for them.

A good example of outreach to the business community is the annual Naval-Industry Research and Development Partnership Conference organized by the Chief of Naval Research, held in Washington on 13–15 August this year. A wide variety of speakers, from both government and industry, spend time exploring business practices and ideas for moving potentially disruptive technologies to fruition.

## Disruption Is Here to Stay

The pace of innovation will continue to increase, and eventually biological revolutions will overlay the information and electronic ones we are experiencing today. The relevance of the sea services as a force in future operations will depend on our ability to identify, develop, and implement—in a word, to manage—such disruptive technology. In the end, we will miss many more times than we hit. Rather than the "single great breakthrough," we more likely will have to manage hundreds of smaller, significant changes. And in the end, the greatest challenge will be letting go of what has so successfully brought us forward to this point. As Admiral Bill Owens has said, "The problem with deep, fast, and rampant innovation is not getting people to accept the new but to surrender the old."[10] Some would say we have difficulty giving up the old because, like a rock climber, we don't have the luxury of letting go with one hand until we have a firm grip with the other: such is the nature of acquisition in the world of national security.[11] But there is room for greater innovation and the taking of a few chances in today's world. We should be prepared to sail against the wind.

## Notes

1. Joseph I. Lieberman, "Techno-Warfare: Innovation and Military R&D," *Joint Forces Quarterly,* Summer 1999, p. 13.

2. Clayton Christensen, Thomas Craig, and Stuart Hart, "The Great Disruption," *Foreign Affairs,* March/April 2001, p. 81.

3. Christensen, Craig, and Hart, "The Great Disruption," p. 85.

4. Christensen, Craig, and Hart, "The Great Disruption," pp. 82–85.

5. Rep. Mac Thornberry, "Using the Past as a Guide for the Future," speech at the American Institute of Aeronautics and Astronautics, 14 February 2001.

6. Andy Krepenevich, Steve Kosiak, Mike Vickers, "The Long Peace," Report by Center for Budget and Strategic Analysis, January, 2001, p. 5.

7. "Road Map for National Security: Imperative for Change," *The United States Commission on National Security / 21st Century,* 15 February 2001.

8. Andy Marshall, remarks to the Defense Science Board, 2 March 2001. For more on Marshall, innovation, and the Navy, see *"The Navy's Dilemma,"* by Tom Hone, U.S. Naval Institute *Proceedings,* April 2001, pp. 75–76, 78.

9. "Road Map for National Security."

10. Adm. William A. Owens, USN, "Revolution in Military Affairs," *Joint Forces Quarterly,* Winter 1995–96. Admiral Owens is former Vice Chairman of the Joint Chiefs of Staff and now co-CEO of Teledesic, a satellite communications firm.

11. Capt. Bill Toti, USN, comments, 13 April 2001.

# PART II

## The Unmanned Revolution

# 7 "A FEW DISRUPTIVE THOUGHTS"

LT Ryan Hilger, USN

As we progress to the second part of this Wheel Book, we turn to take a more detailed look at one particularly disruptive technology that is touching everyone in and out of the sea services: unmanned/robotic systems. In this 2013 Unmanned Maritime Systems Essay Contest Winner, Lieutenant Hilger opens the discussion with a brief look at the fundamental nature of unmanned systems and how they are likely to impact the ways in which operations will be conducted and wars will be fought in the future.

## "A FEW DISRUPTIVE THOUGHTS"

By LT Ryan Hilger, USN, U.S. Naval Institute *Proceedings* (December 2013): 60–65.

Unmanned systems may be the magic bullet the U.S. Navy is looking for, but here are a few points to ponder to keep it from making some costly mistakes.

They burst onto the naval scene with much fanfare only a few short years ago; their collective promise a coveted jewel for maritime commanders, budget hawks, and technology wizards alike. The last two Chiefs of Naval Operations,

Admirals Gary Roughead and Jonathan Greenert, both placed a heavy emphasis on the future role of unmanned systems in the Navy. Speaking at the Association for Unmanned Vehicle Systems International in 2011, Roughead extolled their virtues and decried our inability to get them to the Fleet as quickly as our combat leaders needed, saying the delay "represents, again, a risk-averse culture and an old set of processes that aren't geared to the age in which we live."[1]

Admiral Greenert's most recent directive, his *Navigation Plan*, emphasizes the integration and fielding of unmanned systems across all domains: new munitions for unmanned aerial vehicles (UAVs), small- and large-displacement unmanned underwater vehicles (UUVs), and seamless integration of unmanned payloads for current manned platforms, to name just a few.[2] Other naval and defense leaders clamor for money to field unmanned systems; they seem to be the solution to all of our problems. These systems, they say, will allow us to remove human operators from risk, along with their associated costs, by acting throughout the observe-orient-decide-act-assess (otherwise known as OODAA) loop. But digging beneath the speeches reveals a foundational flaw in the future naval structure—we simply do not understand the full range of capabilities, limitations, and implications of unmanned systems.

## "Repairing the Bedrock"

Repairing the bedrock on which our future naval capabilities may well rest will require a significant course correction—or at least a thorough soul-searching—before we deploy these systems throughout the Fleet. Standing athwart their development, both as student researchers in and future operators of unmanned systems, we need to look beyond the capabilities unmanned systems provide to the strategic, operational, and tactical effects they will produce. That is the real revolution in military affairs. To ensure that the Navy stands ready to dominate in the unmanned battlespace, the Navy should explore how unmanned systems will be employed against us, fundamentally rethink how they can change naval warfare, educate and develop our officer corps to fully exploit their potential, and develop new organizations to produce more rapid technological developments.

Prior to the end of the Cold War, combat seemed like a black and white business. Orders of battle counted the numbers of troops, ships, planes, missiles, and more. The logic went, we have to quantitatively exceed that or develop qualitative force multipliers to compete on a level playing field. First seen two decades ago, on a public scale at least, the U.S. military faced combatants without uniforms, the laws of armed conflict suddenly thrown into confusion. That trend continued throughout the 1990s, reaching its current point in Afghanistan and Iraq.

Intelligence estimates of the enemy became exceedingly hard, making conventional military planning a truly wicked problem. Our adversaries began countering our conventional weapons with improvised explosive devices. The simple technologies and materials needed were widely available to make them an effective weapon against us, forcing us to fundamentally alter our military strategy and adapt our complex, expensive systems to meet the task at hand. As we groped for new and effective strategies for counterinsurgency operations, our enemies continued to wear away our forces. Unmanned systems employed by our adversaries will likely result in the same effects.

## Terrorists' Access

The U.S. government is not the sole entity developing and using unmanned systems. In the coming years, the technology will become increasingly available at lower and lower costs while growing more capable. The non-state combatants who have given us such a hard time over the past decade or more can easily acquire them. A terrorist group could cheaply and easily gain new intelligence-gathering and attack systems with items that could be obtained mostly from Amazon.com: a Parrot AR.Drone 2.0 quadrotor, controlled with an iPhone, costs $300; a GoPro camera, easily mounted to the quadrotor, costs $200. And these people seem to be able to acquire explosives with exceptional ease. Combined with the open-source, Internet-connected sensors around the world, such as Google Maps, oceangoing wave gliders, or the Northeast Pacific Time Series Undersea Networked Experiments (known as NEPTUNE) sonar arrays, for example, adversaries of the United States can significantly close the tactical and operational parity gaps without the need for a leviathan military-industrial complex. The United States must factor this coming reality into the operational concepts of our future forces, both manned and unmanned, to stay ahead of the game.

The development of unmanned systems, from both a military and commercial perspective, will force us to reconsider how we fight, even as we deploy these systems in greater numbers. Our nation-state adversaries are developing unmanned systems at a rapid pace and would benefit greatly from our efforts. A recent event reveals the dark risk of more expensive, military unmanned systems falling into the wrong hands. On 4 December 2011, a stealthy, futuristic, and hitherto unacknowledged drone, the RQ-170 Sentinel, was brought down over Iran intact. Then-Air Force Chief of Staff General Norton Schwartz made several startling, albeit interesting, comments, stating, "There is the potential for reverse engineering, clearly. . . . Ideally, one would want to maintain the American advantage. That is certainly in our minds." He continued, "If [the jet] comes into the possession of a sophisticated adversary, there's not much the U.S. could do about it."[3]

Following that incident, many defense leaders scoffed at the idea that Iran had captured any actual data from the drone; it was designed not to store anything. But that argument is beside the point. A highly advanced unmanned system had fallen into adversaries' hands, giving them the potential for an exponential leap in their own technological efforts. Once the drone is broken into, what would stop Iran from selling the information and technology to our other adversaries, such as China, Russia, or North Korea? China, with its ability to reverse-engineer a system and improve it, could then field our drone designs back against us, strengthening their anti-access/area denial (A2/AD) defenses in Southeast Asia.

## The Name of the Game: "Red Cells"

This case highlights the unintended strategic consequences that unmanned systems will bring to military affairs if we are not careful. Pausing to think about the strategic implications of each new class of unmanned system that we field will yield dividends in the future. To accomplish this, the Navy should stand up "red cells" now to game us. They could explore how unmanned systems will be used against us, how the loss of one of our systems—the RQ-170, for example— would alter the operational and strategic calculus, and thus inform our own developments. The nature of war is immutable. Sun Tzu's adage of "know thy enemy" still applies, and knowing how unmanned systems could be used against us will make us better prepared for the future.

At the operational level of war, unmanned systems will fundamentally alter naval warfare. Admiral Greenert, a few months after taking the helm of the Navy, articulated his vision for the Navy of 2025 in *Proceedings,* emphasizing the side-by-side role that unmanned systems will play with manned platforms. Discussing the undersea domain as an example, he stated,

> With their range and endurance, large UUVs could travel deep into an adversary's A2/AD envelope to deploy strike missiles, electronic warfare decoys, or mines. Smaller UUVs will be used by submarines to extend the reach of their organic sensors, and will operate in conjunction with unattended sensors that can be deployed from surface combatants, submarines, and P-8A patrol aircraft. The resulting undersea network will create a more complete and persistent "common operational picture" of the underwater environment when and where we need it.[4]

The integration of unmanned systems into our naval air and surface forces will be just as complete. Coupled with advances in electronic warfare, to include electromagnetic and cyber warfare, the tools available to a combatant commander will be vastly different from those available today.

To extract every possible advantage that unmanned systems can provide, the Navy must change its mindset from what capabilities the system brings to how we want to fight in the future and how unmanned systems can contribute to that. Consider the following scenario: a U.S. submarine deploys with several UUVs equipped with sonar systems into an A2/AD environment to locate and neutralize a submarine threat. The U.S. commanding officer deploys the UUVs and, after a lengthy search, gains contact on the elusive enemy submarine. Conventional wisdom, training, and doctrine would likely result in our submarine closing to gain sonar contact on her own systems before engaging, possibly even recovering the UUVs first—slow, cumbersome, and somewhat predictable.

Now consider an alternate approach to this tactical problem that shows the required change of mindset. The submarine force, recognizing the potential value of UUVs and the payloads they can carry, alters its tactical-engagement doctrine to use the vehicles in a wholly new and different role. Now the submarine commander deploys the UUVs, equipped with transducers to conduct deception operations in addition to the sonar array, which begin their search. The UUVs gain contact in a short time. The submarine commander does not wait or close range, but instead orders the UUV to disguise itself as an American attack submarine and broadcast sounds of launching a torpedo. The UUV then shifts its disguise to that of an advanced-capability Mark 48 torpedo. The prey, now panicking, does what seems logical by fleeing as fast as possible away from the weapon, right into the jaws of the waiting American submarine, which completes the kill before the enemy realizes what has happened.

## "Two Major Challenges"

Thinking of revolutionary ways to fundamentally alter the way we fight will guide our development of unmanned systems and ensure that they provide the capabilities that will keep the parity gap wide. As bold as the CNO's vision is, transforming it into reality presents two major challenges.

First, the operational-level naval leaders of 2025 are already in service today, mainly as lieutenants and lieutenant commanders. They have already ingested the current service culture, but are still junior enough to accept and help create a new direction if provided with sufficient impetus to do so. The Navy must educate and train these officers on unmanned systems—not just on how to use them, but what they can and, more important, cannot provide to naval warfighters.

At its core, an unmanned vehicle is simply a collection of sensors, communications, propulsion, and potentially weapons. The vehicles are subject to the laws of physics. Assumptions that went into their design have tactical ramifications, such as the accuracy and latency of sensor data or the endurance and persistence of the propulsion system. Officers must be trained to understand the limitations as thoroughly as they understand the specifications and operating characteristics of a gas turbine engine or a nuclear reactor. Simply handing a submarine or destroyer captain a complement of unmanned vehicles with a few technicians to operate them will not develop the broad corporate body of knowledge needed to ensure both the success of the system at that time as well as the future success of these officers as they reach the higher echelons of command.

Officers who completely understand the physical and performance limitations of a particular unmanned system will be able to tactically innovate with those systems, advancing naval warfare further than those who simply employ them as directed with insufficient understanding to question it. To maintain our asymmetric edge at the operational and tactical levels of warfare, the Navy must elevate unmanned systems to the level of a core competency and treat it as such within the Navy's professional military education system.

Second, it takes significantly longer to research and develop a single capability and integrate it into an unmanned system, whether new or existing, than Hollywood tends to portray it. Innovation takes time, especially in a fiscally constrained environment, where research-and-development money is at a premium. The grandiose visions of our senior leaders seem to grasp at this only in a tangential manner, such as Admiral Roughead's previously mentioned indictment in his 2011 speech.

## New Ways to Innovate

The pace of technological development is accelerating in the commercial sector, and the potential for the military to be left behind is quite real. Fixing this process does not require an exponential leap in the evolution of unmanned systems, but rather a fundamental restructuring of how the Navy innovates. A few organizations inform how the Navy could transform its innovation and development processes. The Navy Warfare Development Command has taken a promising first step in breaking the traditional development cycle with the implementation of the CNO's Rapid Innovation Cells (CRIC). Employing the varied education and operational experience of mid-grade officers, CRIC provides selected officers with the means to conduct independent research in emerging technical areas that address urgent naval problems.[5]

The CNO's Strategic Studies Group (SSG), whose primary mission is the development of revolutionary warfighting concepts, operates on a ten-month cycle, with a new cohort of officers entering every year. The SSG has been a hidden hand in guiding the Navy toward development of various naval systems and concepts of operations for almost 20 years, developing some truly revolutionary concepts along the way.

And finally, the Defense Advanced Research Projects Agency (DARPA) operates on a much shorter cycle than most research institutions, and its methodology has enabled it to achieve breakthroughs in record time. Two former DARPA project managers discussed the efficacy of temporary project teams, which "brings together world-class experts from industry and academic to work on projects of a relatively short duration. . . . These projects are *not* (italics original) open ended research programs."[6] Some of DARPA's most notable developments, GPS and micro-electromechanical sensors, for example, were completed in only a year or two.

Combining the best traits of each of these organizations into a new technical-innovation center or program may allow the Navy to achieve a faster pace of capabilities development, which will help keep the tactical and operational advantage firmly on our side. As an additional benefit, the Navy could combine the new innovation concept with the need for officer professional education, thereby allowing officers to rotate through an unmanned systems-innovation cell as a short tour of duty prior to an operational assignment with a heavy unmanned systems component. It would allow officers to see the technical side of system research and development and gain an appreciation for the capabilities of unmanned systems while contributing to the next generation of unmanned capabilities.

Unmanned systems have an incredible potential to revolutionize how we fight and how our enemies fight back. The realization of that untapped potential will only come with a change in our service culture and the full consideration of the implications and limitations that unmanned systems bring, at all levels—technological, tactical, operational, and strategic. The Navy must take steps to educate and develop its officer corps, develop a new and innovative research system, and rethink the role of unmanned systems deployed by us and our adversaries in both peacetime and combat through red cells. These changes must also be conditioned on the rapid technological advances of both our adversaries and the commercial sector, to ensure that we retain our military advantage in all domains and are prepared for the imaginative use of unmanned systems against us. The days of scrimping along with legacy systems and making do with what we have must end. Unmanned systems can usher in the next generation of naval systems and tactics if we want them to. It is time to make the choice.

## Notes

1. ADM Gary Roughead, USN, "Remarks at the 2011 AUVSI Unmanned Systems Symposium and Exhibition on August 19, 2011," www.navy.mil/navy data/people/cno/Roughead/Speech/110819%20AUVSI.pdf.

2. ADM Jonathan Greenert, USN, "CNO's Navigation Plan," www.navy.mil/cno/ Navplan2012–2017-V-Final.pdf.

3. David Majumdar, "Iran's captured RQ-170: How bad is the damage?" *Air Force Times,* 9 December 2011, www.airforcetimes.com/article/20111209/ NEWS/112090311/Iran-s-captured-RQ-170-How-bad-is-the-damage-.

4. ADM Jonathan Greenert, USN, "Navy 2025: Forward Warfighters," U.S. Naval Institute *Proceedings,* December 2011, www.usni.org/magazines/ proceedings/2011–12/navy-2025-forward-warfighters.

5. "Application Period Open for CNO's Rapid Innovation Cell," *Navy Warfare Development Command,* 25 June 2013, www.navy.mil/submit/display.asp ?story_id=75038.

6. Regina E. Dugan and J. Gabriel Kaigham, "Special Forces Innovation: How DARPA Attacks Problems," *Harvard Business Review,* October 2013.

# 8 "DISRUPTIVE TECHNOLOGIES: THE NAVY'S WAY FORWARD"

Robert Morris and CAPT Paul S. Fischbeck, USNR

**In this thought-provoking article,** authors Morris and Fischbeck acknowledge that unmanned systems are here in significant numbers today, and will likely be even more prevalent in the future. They argue that a clear understanding of the capabilities and limitations of these systems is necessary across all segments of the Navy. The authors further postulate that changes may be necessary in the way the service adapts to technological change and in the way it conducts both research and development (R&D) and operational test and evaluation (OPTEV).

## "DISRUPTIVE TECHNOLOGIES: THE NAVY'S WAY FORWARD"

By Robert Morris and CAPT Paul S. Fischbeck, USNR, U.S. Naval Institute *Proceedings* (November 2012): 68–72.

In 2010, the Center for Naval Analyses published "The Navy at a Tipping Point," in which the authors noted that the current force composition was fiscally unsustainable and needed to be altered. They presented several trades that would allow the service to be restructured around future strategic goals.[1] Now, with the projected budget shift to the Pacific, the Navy has more or less implemented those recommendations. Historically, as the CNA authors noted, globally dominant navies have been the leading innovators of their day because they introduced important new classes of ships. Technologically disruptive, those made prior classes obsolete and changed the way navies were organized. Today the era of industrial navies is over, and the time has come for a new kind of Navy.

The Pacific option means the service will abandon some missions in other parts of the world and sail the same types of ships in 2040 as it does today, just fewer of them. But this course of action does not adequately consider the available technological options. Businesses, when faced with such existential challenges, often turn to disruptive technologies—those that allow, even force, fundamental reorganization of the entire enterprise.

For the U.S. Navy in the 21st century, robotic and unmanned systems will create a dramatic reorganization on par with the introduction of steam propulsion or the aircraft carrier. While the Navy and land services have embraced unmanned vehicles in air operations, similar surface and subsurface vehicles have been badly lagging. With less than 1 percent of Department of Defense funding for these types of craft in Fiscal Year 2011, unmanned maritime systems have no fielded programs of record in the Navy's main warfare communities.[2] A learning model adapted from the business world points to how we can mature game-changing technologies quickly and cheaply, while ensuring they meet the requirements to enter the Fleet in large enough numbers to change the Navy's fiscal and strategic future.

The United States is in the best position to invent a dominant naval force of the future. Once it builds the infrastructure to create the future Navy, China and other potential rivals' investments in creating and countering industrial navies will look more like a massive blunder than a threat.

## The Future Force

The authors of the Strategic Studies Group XXVIII report *The Unmanned Imperative* believe this technology and automated networks are the basis of the future Navy. Unmanned systems can provide the naval presence and capability required in coming decades, while remaining within necessary budget limits.

In their capacity as a disruptive technology, they do not represent an improvement on current systems, but rather a new way of organizing. But the new parameters cannot be placed in any existing, proven model, which will emerge only after integrating and operating unmanned technologies. As noted, in the air the Navy is well on its way, with several promising, well-funded programs. But on and under the sea, nobody is currently on track to even discover what measures of effectiveness determine the optimum future force. As much as anyone else, advocates for a legacy-style fleet are guessing based on untested assumptions. Operational experimentation with unmanned systems can provide actual data to develop this force.

The key challenge in introducing disruptive technologies, particularly in the case of unmanned maritime systems, is a lack of "validated learning." All current Navy unmanned maritime vehicle programs assume ship or submarine launching to be necessary—thinking that severely constrains design and choice of propulsion by comparison with shore launching. And yet no operational evidence suggests it is an inferior alternative. The absence of validated assumptions underlying requirements has contributed to repeated failures of Navy unmanned-underwater vehicle (UUV) programs such as the Battlespace Preparation Autonomous Underwater Vehicle and Long-Term Mine Reconnaissance System. This will keep happening until the fundamental suppositions have been examined and corrected, which will lead to positive results.

## How to Validate Learning

In the highly competitive business world, high-tech start-ups' successes at introducing disruptive innovation, particularly in Silicon Valley, come from their ability to generate validated learning quickly and at low cost. They use small-scale operations with real customers, primarily for testing rather than generating profit. These operations test both assumptions about the technology and the accompanying operating model.[3] Based on this information, a start-up quickly modifies the technology, the operational model, or both, to continue the development and test cycle with the newly validated learning. After confirming that both the business model and the technology are viable, the company can scale up. The key difference between this process and that of defense acquisition is that the latter start with a requirement, whereas start-ups begin with an operational hypothesis that gets tested and modified until a profitable model is found.

Weapons are far more difficult to test than Web software, but it is possible for the Navy to verify its assumptions about using unmanned systems with current technology. Employing a validated learning model with naval unmanned systems would speed introduction to the Fleet, mitigate risk, and reduce development and legacy costs. The thought process now in place will eventually produce this learning through hard experience, but if we can get ahead of this mental paradigm instead of being locked into it, we will save time and money and gain an advantage over our competitors.

An example of the type of learning the Navy needs to do in the future is in the development of the RQ-7 Shadow. Despite all the glory that goes to Predator, a substantial portion of all the unmanned aerial-system intelligence on which in-theater action is taken (perhaps better than half) is collected by Shadows. Table 1 shows some of the changes the Army made to Shadow to get it to work. The most important of these were not technical.

The Shadow and its predecessor were originally designed to find Russian air-defense units. Early in the Iraq war, they got misused trying to collect strategic intelligence and failed badly. Shadow units are not set up to support advance planning and high-level coordination for strategic intelligence. However, they are excellent at providing to operational units timely and responsive reconnaissance and targeting information—something with which Predator units can struggle.[4]

From 2002 to 2008, it took the Army hundreds of thousands of combat flight hours to learn all this. There was never a moment when the requirements officer, after being hit with a stroke of genius, created the new validated Shadow needs and displayed it fully formed in a PowerPoint presentation. It takes a long time and a lot of money to make changes to a fielded system, especially when the service did not plan to be modifying it.

Table 1. RQ-7 VALIDATED LEARNING

| FEATURE TYPE | ASSUMED NEED | VALIDATED LEARNING | REASON FOR CHANGE |
|---|---|---|---|
| primary mission | suppression of enemy air defense | reconnaissance, surveillance, & target acquisition | battlefield need matched to capability |
| organizational owner | division | brigade | organizational imperative of mission |
| communication relay capability | HQ | HQ and field unit | new mission needs |
| video relay capability | required | not required but nice to have | lack of new mission need |
| laser pointer | not required | required | new mission needs |
| aircraft life | 100 hours | 1,000+ hours | logistics of new mission |
| fuel type | AVGAS | heavy fuel | logistics of organizational owner |
| mission profile | overt | semi-covert | new mission needs |
| proponent branch | military intelligence | aviation | change of mission and change of ownership |

## The On-Land Experience

The land services took substantial time to figure out how to use unmanned technologies effectively. Many fundamental issues, such as what level of command should have tasking authority, remained unsettled as recently as 2008. Put another way, after a million combat flight hours, the land services still had not worked out the basics of using unmanned technology. The continued introduction of unmanned aircraft with new roles, such as the Army's Grey Eagle and the Air Force's RQ-170, indicates that this learning process is not finished.[5]

The Army and Air Force experience illustrates the magnitude of usage and adaptation required to employ unmanned systems effectively. Not just technology and logistics, but also culture and tactics have to be rewired. Right now, even the best analysts have only an untested notion of what unmanned maritime technology requirements should be. By undertaking serious operations of these systems now, the Navy can speed up the institutional learning process. It is possible for the service to take far less than the million operational hours the Army and Air Force needed to get on top of the learning curve. Key lessons for the Navy's future include the following.

- Unmanned systems are going to play an important role in the force structure, but they are disruptive. They confound requirement writers because their best applications are tactics and missions that are not possible using legacy technologies.
- Gaining real operational experience is much more productive than waiting for technological perfection. In fact, that cannot occur until after extensive operations with imperfect systems.
- The Navy is at the beginning of its learning curve with unmanned systems. It needs to be operating a minimally viable product, not aiming for complete solutions.
- The cultural changes brought by these systems can be brutal.

Data shows that the naval services flew only about one tenth of all unmanned flight hours. This is all the more striking because the Navy–Marine Corps team hours were calculated together. Many of the Marine Corps hours are logged on aircraft that were developed by and for the Army. This means much of the institutional learning about unmanned systems on which the Navy has been relying is outside its department, making it harder to transfer to other maritime domains. Aside from being only at the beginning of its unmanned-systems learning, the Navy lacks what was probably the real impetus for the Air Force's massive funding of unmanned aircraft: through their own increased capabilities in these areas, the other three services and the CIA all were embarrassing it in its core domain. The Navy is, unfortunately, not getting this kind of "encouragement."

The land services have undergone wrenching cultural changes precipitated by unmanned systems, especially the Air Force, which is having a veritable revolution. Distributed operations are challenging the chain of command and traditional control structures. Both in the number of new pilots and in total annual combat flight hours, the UAV component of the Air Force is leading. The service's heroes have changed. The chief of staff is not a fighter or bomber pilot, but comes from the transport community. The sharp tip of the Air Force spear is no longer the F-15 pilot 20,000 feet over the battlefield, but the drone pilot back stateside in an air-conditioned trailer. The Navy will almost certainly have a different experience, but it will probably be nearly as dramatic for important constituencies in the service.

## Not the Hard Way

Better than adapting a fielded system is to field a system that points to what should happen next. The Navy should take advantage of its continuous deployment schedule to create operational experimentation units that work closely with development offices to build a complete solution with promising technology. The mine-hunting UUV programs have employed a user operational-evaluation program, but this needs to be done much more aggressively and in many more mission areas.

Naval researchers have been pushing hard to introduce something beyond oceanographic uses, but systems are not yet operating in the Fleet. Despite funding a UUV energy program and introducing small quantities of mine-hunting craft, widely used unmanned systems are not deployed.[6] These efforts do not match the Navy leadership's rhetoric and will not lead to general-purpose unmanned maritime vehicles being fielded.[7] None of the current technologies on track for acquisition will gather the data and experience necessary to provide future force-structure decision makers with a viable set of options that will address Fleet sustainability issues.

Navy leadership is clear in its desire to have littoral combat ship–deployable unmanned surface vehicles (USVs) and *Virginia*-class-deployable UUVs. This is accompanied by fairly specific notions of size, speed, autonomy, and endurance.[8] Restrictions imposed by the parent platforms severely limit the ability of current technology to do everything the Navy wants. Respectfully, whatever analysis showed this was the best path needs to be rethought, given the capabilities that are truly possible.

Waiting for better batteries or new small-craft physics is a losing game. The Navy must start working with unmanned technologies in real operational environments to figure out its true needs. The service could be operating and testing today at least three alternate approaches to unmanned maritime systems that require no new technology. These operations could inform assumptions about what is needed.

First, large unmanned platforms would offer the speed, power, range, and seakeeping capability necessary to carry operationally useful payloads for core naval missions. The seakeeping, sensors, communications links, and air-breathing power for these platforms are all well understood. Large unmanned vessels also have the size and power to transmit data without using satellites, and over distances that are tactically relevant. However, unmanned vehicles more than 11 meters in length are excluded from the Navy's current USV master plan.[9] If the sensors, weapons, and decision making of an unmanned surface fleet could be independently positioned, a whole new set of tactics would be possible.

Second, shore-based UUVs also present a huge opportunity to bypass subsafe, high-density battery research. The chemistries to make a UUV that will swim from San Diego to Hong Kong and back are no mystery. These fuels are not safe in the confines of a manned submarine, but are well understood as energy sources. However, if UUVs based in Guam or Norfolk can reach anywhere in the world, the need for submarine-deployable vehicles is greatly reduced.

Finally, commercial industry would love to sell the Navy some tiny unmanned vehicles that work as self-assembling sensor networks. These could dramatically change the way naval forces gather tactical information in the maritime domain. They offer the possibility of delivering timely, persistent information about the maritime environment without having a ship or submarine anywhere in the vicinity. Liquid Robotics and iRobot, to name two, have radically different platform offerings ready for purchase in this category. Their products may or may not be what the Navy ultimately wants, but it is not technology that is holding up the deployment of these types of systems.

## Examine the Assumptions

These three paths highlight some of the program assumptions that are constraining current unmanned programs. This is not to say the Navy's current suppositions are wrong, but no OPNAV sponsor or other competent oversight is systematically validating the hypotheses that would give rise to a vibrant and successful unmanned maritime vehicle capability. Table 2 shows how some unfettered thinking could expand the Navy's options. The service's existing vision for unmanned maritime vehicles may be spot on. However, it may also be a technological dead end or a terribly suboptimal method for deploying these craft. Getting operational data is much more useful than debating which position is more expertly reasoned.

All acquisition programs are fraught with risk. There will always be failures, the question is whether they are early and cheap, or are they late in the program, expensive, and troublesome. By using a validated learning model, the Navy can find dead ends quickly and inexpensively. Then acquisition decisions can be based on experience rather than conjecture. Failure and iteration should be a normal part of acquisition. Taking risk at the outset of a project should be encouraged as long as it is systematically tested as soon as possible and appropriate responses are generated. Proceeding to a full development and acquisition program without testing the assumptions about use that underlie the program is a recipe for disaster and an invitation to over-engineering.

The Navy needed to start deploying unmanned maritime technologies yesterday. These first disruptive systems should not be forced into universal adoption, but they must be used to test systematically the assumptions the Navy is making. This will lead to a much clearer understanding of which kinds of technologies the service needs. The Navy can ensure another American century by commencing operation of its unmanned future.

Table 2. UNMANNED MARITIME VEHICLE ASSUMPTIONS
CURRENTLY IMPLICIT IN NAVY PROGRAMS

| FEATURE TYPE | ASSUMED NEED | ALTERNATIVE ASSUMPTIONS |
|---|---|---|
| mission area | mine warfare, ISR, and sometimes submarine warfare | surface warfare, electronic warfare, logistics |
| tactical role | close adjunct to manned ships | independent operations |
| launch | ship or submarine platform | shore launch/ air delivery |
| degree of autonomy required | high (sophisticated mission behavior) | low to medium (constrained mission behavior) |
| vehicle size | suitable for launch platform (LCS or *Virginia*-class capable) | huge to micro (unconstrained or air-droppable) |
| organization | modular detachment | standalone unit/organic |
| mobility requirements | tactically relevant mobility | station-keeping only/ globally self-deploying |
| payload power requirements | kilowatts | watts/hundreds of kilowatts |
| UUV fuel required | rechargeable/ sub-safe | highly volatile high energy fuel |
| USV fueling source | host platform | replenishment oiler/solar/ wave/disposable |

## Notes

1. Daniel Whiteneck, Michael Price, Neil Jenkins, and Peter Swartz, "The Navy at a Tipping Point: Maritime Dominance at Stake?" Alexandria, VA: Center for Naval Analyses, 1 March 2010, ww.cna.org/sites/default/files/researchfthe %20Navy%20at%20e020Tipping%20PoinfY020D0022262.A3.pdf.

2. Department of Defense; "FY 2011–2036 Unmanned Systems Integrated Roadmap, reference no. 11-S-3613, higherlogicdownload.s3.amazonaws .com/AUVSI/958c920a-7f9b-4ad2–9807-f9a4e95d1ef1/UploadedImages

/Unmanned%20Systems%201ntegrated%020Road-map%2OFY2011
–2036%20-%20Final%20-%020Corrected%20Copy.pdf.

3. Eric Ries, *The Lean Start-up* (New York: Crown Business, 2011), theleanstart up.com/.

4. Robert Morris, "Shadow Changes the Game," *Unmanned Systems,* October 2005, 23–27, www.deloitte.com/view/en US/us/Services/audit-enterprise -risk-services/300c7e4085ff6210VgnVCM200000bb4–2f00aRCRD.htm.

5. Dave Majumdar, "Lockheed's New Mystery Drone," Flightglobal /Blogs, June 2012. www.flightglobal.com/blogs/the-dewline/2012/06/lockheeds-new -mystery-drone.html.

6. Office of Naval Research, "Large Displacement Unmanned Underwater Vehicle Innovative Naval Prototype (LDUUV INP) Energy Section Technology," Arlington, VA, August 2011, www.on r. navy. mil/-/media/Files/Funding-Announcements/BAA/2011/11–028-Amendment-0001.ashx.

7. Program Officer Littoral Combat Ship, Program Executive Office website description of remote mine-hunting system, www.acquisition.navy.mil/rda/ home/organizations/peos drpms/peo_lcs/pms_403.

8. ADM Gary Roughead and Peter W. Singer, "The Future of Unmanned Naval Technologies: A Second Look," Washington, D.C., Brookings Institution, March 2011, www.brookings.edu/events/2011/0513_roughead.aspx. See also Raymond Lopez, "Run Silent, Run Long" *Unmanned Systems,* March 2012, 24–28.

9. U.S. Navy, "Unmanned Surface Vehicle Master Plan," Washington, D.C., PEO LMW, July 2007, www.nav.mil/navydata/technology/usymppr.pdf.

# 9 "ΛYE, NAVY ROBOT"

CAPT Danelle Barrett, USN, and CAPT James H. Mills, USN

In Isaac Asimov's classic science-fiction novel *I, Robot,* the author
postulated Three Laws of Robotics, which he considered critical to
maintaining human control over robotic systems with high-order
artificial intelligence (now referred to as "strong-AI"). This clever
article plays on the "Aye, Robot" theme as it considers the likely roles
unmanned systems will play in the sea services and the world at large
in the decades to come. The authors claim that the maturing of
unmanned and autonomous systems will have disruptive yet powerfully positive influences on future naval warfighting.

## "AYE, NAVY ROBOT"

By CAPT Danelle Barrett, USN, and CAPT James H. Mills, USN,
U.S. Naval Institute *Proceedings* (April 2013): 58–63.

Today's Navy is faced with hard choices. In the past, trying times led to innovative
and disruptive improvements in naval warfighting that became game changers,
enabling the United States to prevail in combat. The Navy stands on the cusp
of achieving a huge operational advantage through the use of unmanned and
autonomous systems—air, surface, and subsurface.

However, the current stovepiped legacy approach to design, acquisition, and use of these innovative technologies will prevent the Navy from realizing their full potential. A unified strategy is needed for the future unmanned vehicle (UV) arsenal to achieve an operational advantage and maximize return on investment in a time of increasingly austere military budgets.

Concern is growing for today's Navy to serve as a strategic counterweight to China's regional expansion in the western Pacific and its growing influence across the global commons. Further, there is an escalating sharpness to rhetoric and risk of confrontation with regimes that threaten world and U.S. economic interests as evidenced by Iran's boast to close the Strait of Hormuz, a vital chokepoint necessary to support the world's economic engine. This, combined with more sophisticated transnational terrorist groups, has changed the Navy's operating paradigms.

As the world economy continues to slowly recover from the 2008 recession, the United States and its coalition partners face the economic realities of declining defense spending. However, the requirement for naval services conversely is growing and necessitates a forward-deployed response-and-deterrence presence, thus providing strategic stability in politically volatile regions of the world.

With the aid of technological advances in unmanned and autonomous systems, emerging unmanned, or robotic, systems can deliver stability and power projection in a more responsive and agile way than traditional forces. This will be feasible even with a smaller Fleet. Advances in our nation's research institutions show these unmanned systems can also be autonomous (the ability to perform without continuous human guidance or control). Such autonomy would offer new ways to address complex operational environments. Unmanned systems provide capabilities that would have once required manned aircraft, submarines, or other surface combatants being placed in harm's way or in physically constrained waters.

To support the Department of Defense Unmanned Systems (UxS) Integrated Roadmap, the Navy is increasingly employing aerial, surface, and subsurface unmanned systems (all under the UxS umbrella), primarily in the information domain, for persistent maritime intelligence, surveillance, and reconnaissance (ISR), signals intelligence, support to traditional warfare missions, environmental sensing, and extension of the Navy's net-centric capabilities. Future Navy plans include use of UxS for strike similar to unmanned systems used by other DOD services and agencies.

## "Paving the Cow Path"

This approach offers the economic benefits of riding the bow wave of promising technologies and also gaining an upper hand by using platforms that lower the risk to the human—use machine instead of man in risky operations. However, as the appetite for these capabilities increases and the traditional warfighting communities roll out new systems, they are not aligning effectively to maximize for a combined effect. One critical item lacking is an integrated battlespace framework that links these new platforms with legacy platforms within the Navy and the larger joint/interagency community. By employing these new assets along traditional warfighting lines in an uncoordinated manner, or simply using them as a replacement for missions performed by existing manned vehicles, the Navy is "paving the cow path" and risks losing important operational gains.

There are parallels in this push to employ maritime UxS to the early days of naval aviation. Then, the traditional concepts of naval warfare were challenged to integrate the new implications of manned flight from the sea. Today, the Navy must learn how to align these new unmanned and autonomous systems, not just within the Navy using Navy assets, but inclusive of national, joint, coalition, and interagency UxS platforms as well.

The Navy's future success with UxS depends on its ability to identify effective concepts, integrate operational use, and build the cadre of experts needed to design, acquire, deploy, and operate them within the maritime domain. These are the same challenges faced by naval aviation pioneers like Glenn Curtiss, Theodore Ellyson, Eugene Ely, and Samuel Langley when they trailblazed new military concepts a century ago.

There is a significant "cyber" aspect embedded in successfully delivering UxS capabilities. From an ISR perspective, these robotic systems bring a wealth of resources to the fore but also rely heavily on the operational platform that is the Navy network in order to function and add value. To meet the maritime mission, the robotic systems and the network are symbiotic. Alignment of UxS with network capacity, including space-based assets, is imperative and currently not being done in a holistic manner. This results in faulty assumptions of interoperability and communications capacity that will degrade the total force operational effectiveness and the efficacy of UV platforms. Indeed, these are truly pioneering days from the cyber- and autonomous-technology standpoints.

## The Naval Laws of Robotics

In the classic 1950 novel *I, Robot*, Isaac Asimov laid out the Three Laws of Robotics and wove a storyline that addressed the implications of artificial beings in a human world. Just as this tale considered those implications, we are now at the precipice where the Navy must also consider the consequences of current and emerging unmanned and autonomous systems to both Fleet operations and the traditional concepts of maritime operations.

These ramifications run across many dimensions within the context of naval warfare. Among these are the UxS' impact on sensing and battlespace awareness, participation in maritime kinetic strike, the ability to facilitate the command-and-control (C2) network and the tactical information cloud in action as a cooperative citizen within the Maritime Systems of Systems architecture, and the ability of these robotics systems to fully integrate with manned naval platforms.

## Setting the Course

Similar to Captain Washington Irving Chambers' vision in the pioneering days of naval aviation, when he helped align organizations and efforts toward the common purpose of bringing aviation capability to sea, there needs to be alignment across the Navy's UxS efforts, accountability by designating a warfighting community to lead the combined UxS efforts, and an improved synergy with leading national robotics institutions, research laboratories, and the growing autonomous-systems-engineering industry.

To meet these challenges and to ensure the Fleet is positioned to seamlessly employ these new platforms, several factors must be addressed, primarily the following:

- Unified and indigenous expertise in the technology disciplines that underpin unmanned and autonomous systems is needed. This includes

---

### POTENTIAL NAVAL LAWS OF ROBOTICS:

FIRST LAW: A naval robot must contribute to and integrate with the naval mission and must do no harm to friendly or neutral forces.

SECOND LAW: It must obey its warfare commander and share its sensing information only with those entities its warfare commander designates, except where such orders conflict with the first law.

THIRD LAW: It must protect its own existence as long as this protection does not conflict with the first or second laws or compromise the mission.

---

a requirement for advanced/graduate-level education focused on teaching officers fundamentals on design and employment of UxS for military operations;

- A holistic understanding of systems relationships, operational risk, and technical impacts, including spectrum management, of UxS use within the maritime environment;
- Ensuring a naval force postured to benefit from the research and development communities and commercial expertise in unmanned and autonomous systems;
- A Navy organizationally aligned to explore and quickly act on common issues of UxS across the air, sea, land, and cyber domains.

In assessing all of these factors, it is clear that, as with the advent of carrier-based aviation, a comprehensive strategy coupled with organizational realignments is necessary. The following four emphasis areas are key to getting the Navy on the right vector to better maximize the UxS capabilities and avoid the pitfalls of uncoordinated implementation of complex systems.

*Establish an unmanned and autonomous systems cadre.* The "drivers" of UV platforms should be those officers and enlisted already trained as experts for operating manned platforms in the physical domains; aviators for unmanned aerial vehicles (UAVs); submariners for unmanned underwater vehicles (UUVs);

surface warriors for surface-based UV platforms; and Marines, SEALs, explosive-ordnance-disposal experts, and Seabees for land-based UV platforms. But who are the current Navy's Curtiss, Ellyson, Ely, and Langley of the unmanned and autonomous systems revolution, and who is synchronizing these capabilities across the operational domains?

Today, the Navy is embarking on several UxS programs such as Broad Area Maritime Surveillance (BAMS), Fire Scout, Unmanned Combat Air System (UCAS), Scan Eagle, and several UUV programs. While resource sponsorship is brought together under the Deputy Chief of Naval Operations for Information Dominance (OPNAV N2/N6), the program missions and how they coalesce into the Navy's network and infrastructure are being driven by separate communities and done in an uncoordinated manner along traditional warfighting lines.

This results in duplication of procurement from an acquisition standpoint, operational inefficiencies, and potential unintended interference when deployed. The information-warfare commander at the tactical and operational level of war, working in concert with the other warfare commanders, should serve as the supported commander and take the lead in tactical orchestration of UxS employment. In addition, experts in uniform are needed to look after everything from infrastructure to communications, exploitation to systems interoperability considerations. Without an operationally savvy military cadre focused on these specific UxS implications and skilled in the technical disciplines of computer science, electrical engineering, and systems engineering, it is likely these systems will introduce unintended or disruptive operational consequences.

At a minimum, their potential benefits will be unintentionally marginalized. While there are certainly tactical employment considerations, such as where to employ deconfliction of water space management of UUVs from other vessels or things like altitude deconfliction for UAVs, there are also significant issues in the area of systems interoperability, the ability to transport and exploit ISR or signals-intelligence data, and the need to have assured C2 of these unmanned and autonomous systems. If the Navy fails to bring this expertise together by investing in the appropriate personnel knowledge and skills, it is likely the Laws of Naval Robotics will be violated, resulting in the inability to fully exploit these unmanned and autonomous systems.

*Develop a wholeness perspective on the employment of unmanned and autonomous systems within the naval-warfare construct.* Platforms should be built and used in accordance with an overarching strategy for multi-use—rapidly reconfigurable multimission models for efficiency. For example, a squadron of UAVs on an aircraft carrier should have interchangeable modules that the strike-group commander could rapidly employ depending on the mission. A package could go on the common airframe to perform an ISR mission, a different package to do kinetic or non-kinetic strike, or a communications relay package to extend high-data-rate communications hundreds of miles. This commonality would also be a benefit to minimizing maintenance and training issues.

Early UxS capabilities within the Navy such as the RQ-2A Pioneer or the Tomahawk cruise missile were introduced largely within the confines of a platform-centric viewpoint, focused on relatively narrow surface- or strike-warfare mission scenarios. Each brought with it a support infrastructure and tactics, but the interdependencies on other DOD and Navy systems was not as significant as it is for today's UxS. Largely because of the increasing number of UxS platforms and their reliance on network and communications systems for control, mission guidance, and relay of sensing or other data, there is a significant dependency on the capabilities DOD and the Navy deliver within their global information grid.

This deconfliction and integration cannot be handled with a singular program or platform-centric focus. And UxS development and use must consider ship design, maintenance functions, systems interoperability, spectrum allocation, electromagnetic-interference prevention, manpower and personnel skills, and procedures for safe operation in close proximity to manned platforms (e.g., integration of UAVs within a carrier air wing and water space management of UUVs alongside existing subsurface platforms).

*Form an Unmanned and Autonomous Systems Research and Development (R&D) Consortium.* To date, most UxS systems are being developed and delivered by independent programs and vendors under oversight of individual program offices. While these capabilities are advancing the military capability, the Navy can do more to fully take advantage of the advances in unmanned and autonomous systems that have emerged within the R&D community, and to design architectures that define the interdependencies these systems have within the maritime System of Systems context.

The Navy must ensure it isn't locked into proprietary UxS systems with unforeseen consequences to its technology ecosystem. By establishing an R&D consortium with leading research institutions and industry partners and pushing for multi-use, open-standards-compliant solutions, Navy leadership would have a greatly enhanced perspective on the art of the possible in autonomous-system learning and control, computer vision, more efficient robotics design, better ways to handle the information deluge of sensor data, and advancement in sensor networks.

Such a collaborative endeavor would improve the operational design, architecture, and systems interoperability within the warfighting environment. The Naval Postgraduate School and Naval War College should be key partners in this consortium as well, expanding their relevance by demonstrating their commitment to providing curricula and supporting research in UxS to meet Navy-specific educational requirements.

*Align Man, Train, and Equip Issues.* To better serve Fleet readiness of UxS, the "man, train, and equip" functions should be aligned under a single type commander. This would allow for harmonized advocacy for unmanned and autonomous systems within the Fleet and improved oversight over readiness and interoperability issues. It would also foster unified direction and development of the cadre of UV subject-matter experts who would shepherd these capabilities from concept, to design and delivery, and, finally, to Fleet employment. Such an alignment will allow more efficient use of the Navy's limited UxS expertise and provide a single focal point for UxS Fleet requirements.

The responsible type commander, in coordination with the Naval Warfare Development Command, would coordinate tactics, techniques, and procedures, concepts, and training requirements with the Navy's training, doctrine, and warfare-development community. Traditional schools in each warfighting domain should also revamp their curricula to address the nuances of operating unmanned platforms and their different rules of engagement.

## What Does Compute . . .

While the real assets within the Navy are the talents and initiative of its people, technology does play a significant role. Just as technologies like the catapult, nuclear power, jet propulsion, ballistics computing, satellite communications, networks, and precise navigation and timing have changed naval warfare in the past, the maturing of unmanned and autonomous systems will have disruptive yet powerfully positive influences on future naval warfighting. We must be ready and organize now to capitalize on the operational and fiscal rewards attainable using UV and autonomous-system technology—from sensing to C2 to kinetic operations.

Perhaps it is time to shape the Information Dominance Corps, with its keen understanding of the information domain and foundation in traditional warfighting communities, such that it becomes the lead unrestricted-line community to deliver and amplify the warfighting utility of our emerging unmanned and autonomous systems. As a community that already integrates its core competencies across all warfare areas, becoming the integrators of UV capabilities is a logical progression. It also makes sense to extend the role of the Navy's Cyber Type Commander, Navy Cyber Forces, to have a larger and unifying role in the area of manning, training, and equipping unmanned and autonomous systems.

Those who seek to compete with our national interests and challenge freedom of maneuver on the seas will not hesitate to exploit similar cutting-edge capabilities. The price of unmanned vehicles and autonomous systems is right, the availability plentiful, and their effectiveness proven. The waves of pervasive autonomous-systems technologies in our lives and the deluge of information from persistent environmental awareness are just the beginning. Examples such as robotic vacuums that use antisubmarine-warfare search patterns to navigate our homes or machine learning systems that easily defeat our best TV game-show champions are now taken for granted. We are exposed to more information in a day than our ancestors were in a lifetime. To exploit these trends and achieve a transformational leap in operational superiority, we must unite the Navy's UxS and autonomous-system efforts toward a common strategy, purpose, and vision, and as Asimov noted, make best use of artificial beings in a human world.

# 10 "DRONES TO THE RESCUE!"

Dr. Daniel Goure

**The U.S. Navy's** Unmanned Combat Air System Demonstrator (UCAS-D) wrote a new chapter in naval aviation history when it made an autonomous carrier landing aboard USS *George H. W. Bush* (CVN 77) on 10 July 2013. The X-47B was designed to demonstrate the ability for an unmanned aircraft to successfully operate in the complex environment aboard a carrier and was never intended to be an operational aircraft. In this article, Goure details the way ahead for the follow-on autonomous aircraft which is designated as the Unmanned Carrier Launched Airborne Surveillance and Strike (UCLASS) system. He identifies many of the challenges that must be addressed to capitalize on the potential benefits of a robust autonomous aircraft system.

## "DRONES TO THE RESCUE!"

By Dr. Daniel Goure, U.S. Naval Institute *Proceedings* (September 2013): 34–39.

The current budget squeeze has revived the debate about whether to reduce the number of the Navy's aircraft carriers, but the prospective addition of unmanned aerial vehicles to the flattop's arsenal will make the ships even more valuable in coming years.

When the X-47B *Salty Dog 502* became the first drone to land on an aircraft carrier in July, Navy officials properly hailed the event as a technological milestone. Not only did the unmanned aerial vehicle (UAV) catapult from the flight deck of the USS *George H. W. Bush* (CVN-77) and successfully perform touch-and-go exercises and two landings, catching the tailhook wire with precision, but it did all of that autonomously, using its own robot "brain" of complex algorithms without need of a human drone operator as most other UAVs require. "It's not often you get a chance to see the future, but that is what we got today," Secretary of the Navy Ray Mabus declared after the demonstration.

But the success of the X-47B landing marked more than just a technological achievement; it also injected a new element into the recently revived strategic debate over how many aircraft carriers the Navy will need in coming years. As part of an advanced surveillance-and-strike system that the Navy is developing, drones will soon be able to conduct long-range, 'round-the-clock intelligence-gathering missions and aerial attacks that will make carriers cheaper to build, less costly to operate, and far more effective, and will spawn radical changes in the way the Navy uses them. As a result, the addition of the drone to the naval aviation carrier force may prove to be a major factor in saving the flattop from becoming an endangered species.

The issue is important because, as anyone who has been following the recent budgetary developments in Washington knows, the future of the carrier is under increasing stress. Critics have contended that the Navy's longstanding strategy of building the Fleet around a core of 11 nuclear aircraft carriers is becoming too expensive, and that the concept has been unable to keep pace with the rapidly growing array of threats from potential adversaries. And with the retirement of aging aircraft systems such as the A-6 and the S-3, some say the overall striking power of the carrier air wing has declined.

Indeed, Secretary of Defense Chuck Hagel disclosed on 31 July that one of the largest potential spending cuts that a "strategic choices and management review" panel suggested earlier this year was to reduce the number of carrier strike groups from the current 11 to a new level of only eight or nine. "The basic tradeoff is between capacity . . . and our ability to modernize weapons systems and to maintain our military's technological edge," the secretary said.

## Why the Drone Landing Mattered

It's here that the X-47B's mid-July milestone was especially significant. The drone was developed as part of the Navy's effort to design and test a UAV-centered unmanned combat air system. During the week that the *Bush* demonstration was being conducted, the Navy invited four defense contractors to submit preliminary design studies for an unmanned carrier-launched airborne surveillance and strike system, known as UCLASS. The Navy's hope is to conduct an open competition in Fiscal Year 2014 that will result in the deployment of an operational system by FY 2020.

The key performance parameters set out in the Navy's invitation answered several lingering questions about the operational concept for UCLASS. The system's primary role will be to conduct long-distance intelligence-gathering, surveillance, and reconnaissance (ISR), and to improve targeting. According to published documents, the UCLASS system must be able to conduct two unrefueled orbits at 600 nautical miles or one unrefueled orbit at 1,200 nautical miles. In lightly contested environments, it must be able to conduct strike missions out to 2,000 nautical miles. The drone must be able to lift a 3,000-pound payload, made up primarily of sensors but including 1,000 pounds of air-to-surface weapons such as the 500-pound Joint Direct Attack Munitions (JDAMS) and the Small Diameter Bomb II. Even with such capabilities, contractors will have to keep the price-tag for UCLASS under $150 million, not including items such as sensor packages, weapons, spare parts, and training.

The modest performance parameters indicate that, despite the potential, once the UCLASS system gets off the ground, the Navy will take a cautious, step-by-step approach. The focus on the ISR and light-attack missions means that UCLASS drones do not require high speed, extreme agility, or even stealth features. This, in turn, will simplify design and production and, in a time of growing austerity, reduce cost. Just as important, the UCLASS will fill a significant void in carrier-based long-endurance/long-distance ISR, essentially doubling the duration of these operations. The limited air-to-ground capability envisioned for the UCLASS drone means that it will supplement—but not replace—the primary strike force of the carrier air wing, the F/A-18 E/F (and soon the F-35C as well).

As currently envisioned, the new system will be only a small step toward defining the carrier air wing of the future. But if it succeeds and is expanded, UCLASS—and the systems that follow it—could prove to be important elements in the debate over future missions for the modern aircraft carrier and how many CVNs to retain in the Fleet.

## Reviving the Debate

It's been a long time since there was a serious discussion about the future of the aircraft carrier. Yet, with growing frequency and intensity, Navy strategists (and periodicals such as *Proceedings*) have been questioning the central place given to the CVN in Navy strategy and shipbuilding plans.[1]

The issue that has drawn the greatest attention is how vulnerable critics say the aircraft carrier has become in the face of a number of emerging threats. China has developed new antiship ballistic missiles with guided warheads, which seem designed to target large naval vessels such as carriers.[2] And potential U.S. adversaries have acquired a raft of new weapons for anti-access and area-denial (A2/AD) operations, from manned aircraft and sea-skimming cruise-missiles that can be delivered from land, sea, or air to diesel-electric submarines. Taken together, the critics contend, these will place the United States' entire surface Navy at greater risk and force the carrier strike group to take additional protective measures that could include operating farther from hostile shores or even restricting overall offense operations significantly.[3]

A second issue, which has gained greater prominence in the face of congressional calls for deep defense spending cuts, is the cost of naval aviation—from building and maintaining aircraft carriers to deploying their air wings and supporting vessels. The soaring cost overruns and construction delays in the production of the USS *Gerald R. Ford* (CVN-78), the first of a new class of Navy super-carriers, have raised concerns both within the Navy and on Capitol Hill.[4] At the same time, the cost of the carrier air wing is rising visibly even though it is shrinking in size.[5] Navy leadership and a number of outside experts have offered a spirited defense of the *Ford*-class carriers.[6]

The third challenge—and the most central for the future of the UCLASS drone and its successors—is that of making sure that the future carrier air wing

(CVW) is effective. Early assessments of the potential for UAVs to enhance the utility of the carrier air wing focused on the value of their greater range and persistence.[7] As Representative J. Randy Forbes (R-VA), chairman of the House Armed Services subcommittee on seapower and projection forces, has argued, the issues of reach and persistence remain the most serious weaknesses of the CVW—particularly in the face of the Obama administration's new, more intense focus on Asia.

> [T]he long distances in the region, combined with A2/AD challenges, raise questions about the future strike power of the Carrier Air-Wing (CVW). As we posture our forces, is the planned CVW of the 2020s structured to meet the range, persistence, stealth, ISR, and payload demands that will be required to operate in this theater?[8]

## Up in the Air

The CVW of the near-future also is in flux. The F/A-18 E/F will play a significant role in both air-to-air and air-to-ground missions for the next several decades. The F-35C, long styled as the eventual centerpiece of the air wing, soon will be deployed. The EF-18G Growler is on the decks and will be upgraded with the Next-Generation Jammer. The Navy plans to acquire 75 E-2D Advanced Hawkeyes, which provide a leap forward in airborne ISR and networked fire control, but production of these is slowing. Finally, the MH-60R will provide a substantial increase in the CVW's antisubmarine warfare capabilities.

Yet, if UCLASS is to be anything more than a show horse, it must pull its weight in the continuing evolution of the CVW. This means that its designers will have to address some of the challenges facing the carrier and the air wing and also set the stage for exploiting the full potential of the new *Ford*-class CVN.

The Navy's invitation to contractors clearly is designed to produce a UCLASS drone system that will be a workhorse for the CVW. In its ISR role, UCLASS will significantly expand the carrier strike group's ability to see, assess, and respond to threats. This is of particular importance in the context of the Asia-Pacific pivot as well as the proliferation of longer-range antiship missiles. Equally important,

UCLASS will make it possible for a single air wing to conduct 'round-the-clock air and maritime surveillance. Finally, in its light-attack role, UCLASS will expand both the reach and flexibility of the air wing, allowing the more capable F/A-18 E/Fs and F-35s to be employed where their advanced features are most appropriate. The ability of the UCLASS to loiter while carrying heavier weap ons than a Hellfire missile will be especially valuable in low-intensity conflicts, where exquisite precision strikes have become the norm.[9]

Flexibility will be another important attribute for the winning UCLASS design. Given rapid advances in sensors, weapons, and networking, the UCLASS needs to have inherent flexibility and some room for growth to allow the carrier air wings to experiment with it and incorporate lessons learned from the system's initial employment.

Over the longer-term, for the current challenges to the continuation of the aircraft carrier as the Navy's primary ship, designers of the UCLASS will have to integrate the new program into the operational policies of the carrier air wing and exploit the inherent strengths of the *Ford*-class CVNs. In his speech marking the successful carrier landing of the X-47B, Navy Secretary Mabus suggested how unmanned systems will address all three of the challenges to the aircraft carrier.

> The operational unmanned aircraft that will follow it will radically change the way presence and combat power is delivered from aircraft carriers by conducting surveillance and strike missions at extreme distances and over very long periods of time. With this advanced technology, we will put fewer sailors and Marines in harm's way, and we will push the area of potential action even farther from the decks of our ships.
>
> And it's more efficient. Because unmanned carrier aircraft do not require flights to maintain pilot proficiency, they will deploy only for operational missions, saving fuel costs and extending the service life of the aircraft.
>
> Not only will future carrier air wings be more combat-effective, they will cost less to build, and having less-expensive airframes means

we can build more and use them differently, like developing swarm tactics and performing maneuvers that require more G-force than a human body can withstand.[10]

Other observers have gone even further, suggesting that the success of the UCLASS effort would not only radically alter how the CVW operates, but would change the character, mission, and roles of the carrier itself. The next-generation UCLASS drone will have to have a range equal to that of the current proposed design, but it also will have to carry a significantly larger payload and have the ability to deploy long-range air-to-ground weapons. This would allow the CVW to engage targets at or beyond the range of current and projected antiship ballistic and cruise missiles. A large payload capacity could also allow the UCLASS to fill a yawning gap in current CVW capabilities—air-to-air refueling of both manned and other unmanned platforms.[11]

It is also worth observing that none of these missions requires a high degree of autonomy, the Holy Grail for many advocates of accelerated deployment of unmanned aerial systems. Complex missions will remain the domain of manned systems for decades to come.[12]

Ultimately, future generations of UCLASS drones may need to incorporate stealth characteristics as well. However, by that time weapons-makers may have developed an entirely new means of detecting and cloaking airborne systems. And it's no longer clear whether we should be focusing our efforts to improve capabilities and tactics to counter A2/AD threats on the platform or on the payload. As a result, it would be a mistake to embark on the design of a next-generation stealthy UCLASS drone system prematurely.

## A *Ford* in the Carrier's Future?

Even so, it's possible to envision exploiting the design improvements in the *Ford*-class carrier, with its tremendous interior volume and enormous power-generation capability, to help turn nuclear aircraft carriers into mother ships for swarms of unmanned aerial systems and long-range missiles. One aspect of such an evolution would be to pursue options for designing future unmanned aerial systems so as to introduce entirely new ways of conducting operations aboard flattops that would permit carrier air wings to launch more sorties with fewer people. That would be a big plus as well.[13]

All of these are complex challenges, and it doubtless will take time, effort, and a lot of experimentation to engineer the kind of UCLASS technology that will fit the Navy's needs—and a timetable for deploying it throughout the carrier force. But the demonstration on board the *Bush* does show clearly that the drone can enhance air operations at sea in a way that wasn't envisioned even a decade ago and that hasn't yet been fully appreciated either by the Navy as a whole or by civilian policymakers.

When it is, the aircraft carrier will get a new lease on life.

## Notes

1. Michael O'Hanlon and Bruce Reidel, "Land Warriors: Why the United States Should Open more Bases in the Middle East," *Foreign Affairs,* 2 July 2013, and a rejoinder by Stacie Pettyjohn and Evan Braden Montgomery, "By Land and By Sea: Balanced Forces for a Complex Region," *Foreign Affairs,* 19 July 2013. CAPT Henry J. Hendrix, USN, "At What Cost a Carrier?" Center for a New American Security, Washington, DC, March 2013. CAPT Robert Rubel, USN (Ret.), "The Future of Aircraft Carriers," *Naval War College Review,* Autumn 2011.

2. Bill Gertz, "China has carrier-killer missile, U.S. admiral says," the *Washington Times,* 27 December 2010. Rebecca Grant, "A Specter Haunts the Carrier, *Air Force Magazine,* vol. 92, no. 12, December 2009. Ronald O'Rourke, "China Naval Modernization: Implications for U.S. Navy Capabilities—Background and Issues for Congress," Congressional Research Service, CRS Report RL33153. Loren B. Thompson, "Can China Sink a U.S. Aircraft Carrier?" *Forbes,* 23 January 2012.

3. Anthony H. Cordesman, Ashley Hess, and Nicholas S. Yarosh, "Chinese Military Modernization and Force Development: A Western Perspective," Center for Strategic and International Studies, Washington, DC, 25 July 2013. LTC Andrew F. Krepinevich, USA (Ret.), "Why Air-Sea Battle?" Center for Strategic and Budgetary Assessments, Washington, DC, 2010.

4. O'Rourke, "Navy Force Structure and Shipbuilding Plans: Background and Issues for Congress," Congressional Research Service, CRS Report RL32665, 3 July 2013, especially 18. Tony Capaccio, "Aircraft Carrier's Cost

Draw U.S. Lawmakers' Concern," *Bloomberg News,* 21 May 2013. O'Rourke, "Navy Ford-Class (CVN-78) Aircraft Carrier Program: Background and Issues for Congress," RL20643, Congressional Research Service, April 19, 2013.

5.  Hendrix, op, cit.

6.  Kris Osborne, "Navy Leaders Defend Ford-Class Carrier Program," *Military. com,* 30 April 2013.

7.  Thomas P. Ehrhard and Robert O. Work, "Range, Persistence, Stealth, and Networking: The Case for a Carrier-Based Unmanned Combat Air System," Center for Strategic and Budgetary Assessments, Washington, DC, 2008.

8.  Randy Forbes, "Questioning the 2020 CVW," June 2012 at blog.usni.org /2012/06/22/questioning-the-2020-cvw.

9.  David Deptula, "Drones Best Weapons We've Got For Accuracy, Control, Oversight; Critics Don't Get It," *Breaking Defense,* 5 February 2013.

10. Secretary of the Navy Ray Mabus, "Technology on Approach: Unmanned aircraft at sea greatly extend the Navy's reach and sustainability," *San Diego Union-Tribune,* 12 July 2013.

11. Forbes, "What is the potential and what are the challenges the Navy faces in fielding a UCLASS to the fleet?," 28 June 2012, at http://www.information dissemination.net/2012/06/what-is-potential-and-what-are.html.

12. Daniel Taylor, "Beyond Drones," *Seapower,* vol. 56, no. 7, July 2013.

13. Osborne, "Future Carriers Built to Carry Drone Fleets," *DefenseTech.org,* 19 July 2013.

# 11 "HOW TO FIGHT AN UNMANNED WAR"

LT James E. Drennan, USN

We all anticipate that our brightest scientists and engineers will provide future warfighters with sensors and weapons of the types only
seen previously within the pages of science fiction novels. They have
already delivered highly capable robots and high-energy lasers that
are remarkable, but they should only be considered the "Model-As"
of their breed. In the article that follows, Lieutenant Drennan asks
how tactics will be developed to effectively utilize the power to be
unleashed by unmanned and robotic systems. He wonders if there
could ever be an "unmanned war," and if so, how should we fight it?

## "HOW TO FIGHT AN UNMANNED WAR"

By LT James E. Drennan, USN, U.S. Naval Institute *Proceedings*
(November 2010): 58–62.

Imagine this future scenario: The United States is on the brink of war with a
hostile state threatening national security. But we have a military option that
will not risk the life of a single American Soldier and will protect countless
innocent civilians. The President can deter nuclear war and avoid a bloody
invasion with a single order: Send in the drones.

Unmanned fighter jets launch from aircraft carriers and conduct bombing runs on the enemy's military infrastructure. Autonomous ground vehicles seek out and destroy their forces, which have already been tracked remotely by satellite. At sea, as the enemy launches a submarine campaign against merchant shipping while mining critical waterways, a network of autonomous undersea vehicles responds by locating submersed threats and strategically self-destructing to neutralize the danger.

As a last-ditch effort, the enemy launches its entire arsenal of nuclear weapons—but the missiles are immediately knocked out of the sky by directed-energy lasers, before their warheads are armed. When the conflict moves into a counterinsurgency phase, specialized drones—equipped with facial-recognition technology, electronic-warfare and improvised-explosive-device-detection capabilities, and offensive weaponry—disrupt and dismantle the rebellion to clear the way for security forces.

When the smoke clears, the campaign is hailed as one of the most decisive and humane victories in the history of warfare. Zero American casualties, and zero innocent civilians killed. The advantages of such a campaign are clear, but many technical questions need to be addressed before the U.S. military can fight a war almost entirely with robots.

Still, the most important concerns are not the technical problems involved with robotics design and development. Talented engineers, technicians, and computer programmers are finding solutions on a daily basis. The military must first assess the impact of robotics on tactics before it can effectively wield such a revolutionary weapon.

Who will be the tacticians in robotic warfare? When and where will tactical decisions be made? How will the tactics change? Why is robotic warfare really being pursued? The answers to these questions illuminate the path to victory in this type of warfare. But without sufficient control and understanding of the tactical paradigm shift, the results of robotic warfare could be far worse than the scenario described here.

## Who Is the Tactician in Robotic Warfare?

In conventional warfare, a major offensive requires a multitude of tacticians, including aircraft, ship, and ground commanders. Tactical decisions are made on the spot by all grades and ranks of warfighters as well. In general, the tactical decision-making process of this military involves closely linked decisions and actions. Rarely is there any ambiguity as to who makes tactical decisions.

In robotic warfare, the tactician is not so obvious. Different levels of automation introduce different decision makers into the process. At the lowest level of automation, remotely piloted vehicles (RPVs) are controlled directly by human operators. Currently, most RPVs are aircraft, so the operators are predominantly pilots. As the use of robots becomes more prevalent, however, non-pilots will increasingly have tactical control of robots. As actual combat experience becomes rarer, these newcomers to the tactical process will have to rely on their training to ensure their combat effectiveness.

At the highest level of automation, i.e., artificial intelligence (AI), the robot itself would be the tactician (and possibly the strategist). However, the potential military application of AI involves complex issues that are beyond the scope of this article. Slightly less-autonomous robots—which are programmed to make tactical decisions on their own without the need for a human operator—are rapidly gaining in both popularity and technological maturity. In this case, the tactician is neither the operator nor the robot, but the programmer. Given a particular scenario or set of inputs, code within the machine will predictably produce the outcome the programmer intended.

But without a solid foundation of tactical expertise, the commander's intent could give way to the programmer's intent. Regardless of the level of automation, robotic warfare will rely on the tacticians, whoever they may be, just as much as does conventional warfare.

## Where Is the Tactical Decision Made?

Robotics will change more than just who makes decisions in warfare. Such a revolutionary capability can impact the battlespace itself. For example, when soldiers acquired rifled gun barrels in the 19th century, their accuracy increased so much that they were able to decimate advancing armies from a safe distance. The battlefield was forever expanded and dispersed. In the early 20th century, the advent of submarines introduced an entirely new dimension to the maritime battlespace.

Similarly, robotics will forever change the tactical nature of the battlespace. In robotic warfare, the critical point of decision in the tactical process is moved physically farther from the point of action than ever before. In the case of RPVs— robots with no autonomy—the tactical decision-maker will not be on the battle-field, or even necessarily in the theater. He or she will be in a secure control center half a world away, far removed from combat both geographically and psychologically.

This vast separation between decision and action requires tremendous mental discipline and concentration. Already examples of the contrary are producing disastrous results. In October 2009, an Air Force Predator drone crashed into a mountain in Kandahar, Afghanistan, because the flight crew, who had just taken the watch at an air reserve base in California, was preoccupied with a major battle occurring below.[1] When unmanned aerial vehicles crash, the fact that no pilot was killed is often highlighted. In this case, however, the distributed nature of the command system and lack of close tactical control contributed to the disaster. An onboard pilot may have been fatally injured in the crash, but it is hard to believe that he or she would not have been able to avoid that mountain in the first place.

A far more tragic example occurred in February 2010, when an Army helicopter killed 23 Afghan civilians after an Air Force Predator drone crew based in Nevada incorrectly identified them as insurgents. In the investigation report that followed, Major General Timothy McHale condemned the crew's communication as "inaccurate and unprofessional" and stated that vital information, such as the presence of children, was downplayed to the ground commander. Additionally, McHale cited a lack of "insights, analysis, or options" from command posts in Afghanistan to the ground commander.[2] The Predator drone crew, as well as analysts at the in-country command posts, failed to hold themselves to the high standard required by combat operations.

Even with experienced pilots and tacticians controlling RPVs, overcoming the challenges introduced by the geographical separation of decision and action remains difficult. Yet the military is increasingly training non-pilots to operate the aircraft. Furthermore, mission operators are frequently junior personnel—

most likely lacking combat experience as more and more robotics are used—whose training is focused on the technical aspects of operating the machine.

To be effective in the long term, they must be given the extensive tactical training given to the aircraft, ship, and ground commanders of today's military. Manpower and training are not areas of cost savings, particularly in the context of RPVs. It is already becoming evident that the tacticians of robotic warfare require at least the same standard of training—and compensation—as do tacticians of conventional warfare. The expanded battlespace resulting from the separation between point of decision and point of action only raises that standard.

## When Is the Tactical Decision Made?

On the other end of the autonomy spectrum from RPVs are autonomous robots capable of making tactical decisions on their own. The military application of these robots continues to gain interest because of their ability to process information much more abundantly and rapidly than can a person. While a human operator is just starting the tactical decision-making process, a robot evaluates millions of possible scenarios and selects the decision that produces the best outcome. This level of automation has the potential to mitigate risk by quickly and decisively waging war, while minimizing the probability of error.

But there are consequences for using fully automated robots. They do not have AI, but rather they are preprogrammed with tactical decision-making capabilities that enable them to operate in combat without direct control from an operator. Essentially, the decisions themselves are made in advance by skilled programmers who anticipate a wide range of stimuli.

This dynamic is fundamentally no different from that of a chess supercomputer designed to compete against a grandmaster. For example, IBM's Deep Blue defeated world champion Garry Kasparov in 1997 by processing 200 million positions per second, analyzing a database of historical master games, and using algorithms that model master chess play.[3] Since all of its decisions came from code written by IBM's team of programmers and grandmasters, Deep Blue's moves could, theoretically, have been predicted by examining the code within the machine. Nevertheless, Deep Blue was able to defeat a world champion by combining processing power with tactical expertise. IBM's victory is often credited to "brute force," i.e., the computer's ability to quickly consider every possible scenario up to 20 moves deep. However, without the grandmasters' tactics, which were decided before the match was played, Deep Blue would have been doomed to failure against a world-class opponent like Kasparov.

Interestingly, as processing technology advanced over the next decade, the focus in computer-chess research actually shifted from processing power to chess tactics. In 2006, a PC-based chess program capable of processing only 8 million positions per second defeated world champion Vladimir Kramnik.[4] Victory was achieved through advanced heuristics and algorithms, not raw processing power.

Just as IBM invested in the tactical expertise of chess grandmasters, the military must invest in experienced tacticians and tactical training for computer programmers. The job of the tactician here is extremely difficult, because not only must the decisions be made far from the battlefield, they must also be made long before the battle even begins. Every line of code must be written with an eye toward the tactical outcome it is intended to produce.

Injecting a human supervisor into the decision-making process does allow some tradeoff between decision quality and time management. A supervisor can safeguard against obviously poor decisions much closer to the point of action, but the advantage of near-instantaneous decision-making is lost. In the heat of battle, that tradeoff may not even be an option. In any event, most decision-making still occurs before the battle. If an assistant had moved the chess pieces for Deep Blue and only intervened if the computer was playing into a checkmate, would the assistant have been crowned world champion?

## How Will Robotic Warfare Change Tactics?

By focusing on the people involved in robotic warfare, the military can successfully navigate the changing tactical landscape in pursuit of victory. Excellence through tactical training will provide a compass, but the exact route will be discovered over time through experience and ingenuity. While specific tactics in robotic warfare are yet to be determined, tactical principles and the unique capabilities of robotics point to some potential areas of focus for research.

- *Resistance to radiological, biological, and chemical warfare:* The effects of these attacks, while often fatal to human warfighters, pose little danger to robots. While civilians are susceptible to these types of weapons, robotic warfare can diminish their utility.

- *Distributed command:* In conventional warfare, the loss of a battlefield commander can introduce chaos and lead to defeat. In robotic warfare, there is no such commander for the enemy to target. Even if a commander is using one particular robot and it is destroyed, the command function can be transferred to the next available machine.

- *Removal of human emotion on the battlefield:* Even the most courageous warfighters take cover from suppressive fire or suffer shellshock from nearby explosions. Human nature has always governed the dynamics of battle, but robots are not subject to emotions such as fear and intimidation. Conversely, an army of unwavering advancing robots can be a daunting sight to an enemy force.

Not only will robotic warfare change the tactics of the military with the machines, but the military facing them will also be forced to reevaluate the way it fights. Just as robots will precipitate changes in tactics based on their capabilities, certain vulnerabilities will provide opportunities on which the enemy can focus its tactics.

- *Electromagnetic pulse:* The radiological effects of nuclear weapons may not be harmful to robots, but another side effect—electromagnetic pulse—could be detrimental. A nuclear weapon's ability to damage and/or destroy electrical systems could make it the preferred method of attack against a robotic military.

- *Cyber warfare:* Though still maturing, cyber warfare is more advanced than robotic warfare, and since robots depend heavily on computer networks, they will be a prime target. By infiltrating key networks, an enemy could quickly debilitate large numbers of robots or, much worse, hijack them and turn them against friendly targets.

- *Psychological operations:* Enemies will be able to capitalize on any mistakes made by robots, especially the killing of innocent civilians. By painting robotic warfare as heartless and cowardly, enemies can rally public opinion—both local and American—if it is not conducted at the highest standards.

- *Targeting of command centers:* Command centers and any other command-and-control nodes will become prime targets because, aside from their traditional value, without them many robots will cease to function. One attack on a command center can effectively defeat thousands of robots on the battlefield. With many such centers located on American soil, attacks on the homeland will become more common.

## Why Is Robotic Warfare Being Pursued?

To determine if victory can even be achieved primarily using robots, the motivation behind this type of warfare must be clarified. What capability gaps are these machines intended to fill? Obviously, the introductory scenario represents an unattainable ideal of zero-error warfare; however, the capabilities described can approach that ideal. Furthermore, all the technologies in the scenario are either being researched or currently fielded. The potential for risk mitigation to combat personnel is already displayed by the unmanned systems in operation today, while advancements in computer-processing power continue to reduce the probability of collateral damage. Nevertheless, several other motivations for developing robotic-warfare capabilities are often cited. These include the following.

Some believe that unmanned vehicles could reduce manpower requirements. On the contrary, the military is learning that robotic warfare only displaces the manpower requirements. A typical drone crew consists of a pilot, a camera operator, and an analyst—not to mention a distributed network of analysts and controllers to ensure that raw data is relayed and processed into relevant intelligence.[5] Only when the military is willing to hand over tactical control to fully autonomous robots will manpower requirements truly be reduced.

Another reason for which robotic technology is often touted is the improved mission profile allowed by not having a human located on the platform. For example, removing the person alleviates the constraint on mission duration set by human fatigue and frees up around 200 pounds of payload. Yet these factors should be considered benefits, not motivators, of robotic warfare. Since reliability and maintainability of combat aircraft, particularly in hostile environments, have not fundamentally improved just by removing the pilot, failure rates will still affect mission endurance.

Meanwhile, if additional payload were the prime motivator, the military would have invested at least $50 million per pound of payload per platform, based on a conservative estimate of a $10 billion total DOD investment in unmanned vehicles to date.[6] This seems a high price to pay.

So, while robotics may offer myriad tactical benefits, their capability to mitigate risk to American warfighters and civilians should provide the central motivation for their advancement. Eventually, when the technology has sufficiently matured, victory achieved through the use of robotics will not only be possible, but plausible. Robotics can have a game-changing impact on par with guided munitions or nuclear weapons. Enemies of the United States have learned over the past few decades that sapping the American public's will to fight can be an effective strategy. But if they are faced with an assault that effectively eliminates the hazard to American soldiers and innocent civilians, enemies will surely question that strategy.

## What's the Worst That Can Happen?

If the military does not grasp control of the tactical challenges of robotic warfare, the results could be disastrous. Consider a different scenario of robotic assault from the one introducing this article. This time, operators of unmanned fighter jets fail to fly tactical ingress and egress routes. Their lack of tactical expertise makes their aircraft easy targets for enemy air defenses. Autonomous ground vehicles cannot overpower unscathed enemy air and ground forces, necessitating a conventional invasion. At sea, an American warship is sunk by an autonomous undersea vehicle whose command-and-control network has been taken over by enemy hackers.

Counterinsurgency drones massacre an entire village during a festival, because they mistake costumed civilians for combatants and fireworks for gunfire. Instead of launching nuclear missiles, the enemy detonates its nuclear weapons within its own borders to incapacitate the remaining robots. Hundreds of thousands of innocent civilians are killed in the process. Aside from the military defeat and terrible loss of human life, much of the capital invested in robotic technology would have been wasted in this scenario, because the American public would never again condone robotic warfare.

In fact, the acceptable limits of error will be much lower in robotic warfare. The rapid technological advancement of the past several decades has shown that as the margin of error diminishes, so does the user's tolerance for error. In the public's mind, new achievements become standards, and goals become expectations. It will be the responsibility of tacticians to meet those expectations.

With all of the revolutionary implications of robotics in warfare, they are still just like any other weapon in one very important respect. As with any weapon, the true power of robotics ultimately comes not from the capability of the weapon itself, but from the warfighter's ability to effectively wield that weapon.

## Notes

1. "UAV Crash Blamed on Distraction of Battle," *Air Force Times*, 5 April 2010.
2. David Zucchino, "U.S. Report Faults Air Force Drone Crew, Ground Commanders in Afghan Civilian Deaths," *Los Angeles Times*, 29 May 2010.
3. Monty Newborn, *Kasparov versus Deep Blue: Computer Chess comes of Age* (New York: Springer, 1997).
4. "Chess Champion Loses to Computer," BBC News, 5 December 2006, http://news.bbc.co.uk/2/hi/europe/6212076.stm.
5. Zucchino, "U.S. Report Faults Air Force Drone Crew."
6. Government Accountability Office, *Defense Acquisitions: Opportunities Exist to Achieve Greater Commonality and Efficiencies among Unmanned Aircraft Systems* (Washington, DC: GAO, 2009).

# 12 "UNMANNED, UNSEEN, AND UNDER THE SEA"

LCDR Brent Johnson, USN, and VADM John Richardson, USN

Through always-engaging video on the evening news and a never-ceasing flood of political cartoons, we are all well aware of the ways in which unmanned aircraft (usually called drones) have been used to fight terrorists around the globe. Many observers also know about the ubiquitous ground robots that have saved so many lives in the explosive ordnance disposal (EOD) field. Little is known, however, about the R&D efforts being conducted in the area of Unmanned Undersea Vehicles (UUVs), which are sometimes alternately referred to as Autonomous Underwater Vehicles (AUVs). The incredibly difficult constraints of the undersea environment make communications between the vehicles and their controllers nearly impossible, and extreme hydrostatic pressure at ocean's depths allows little margin for error. Despite these difficulties, research is well underway on Large Diameter Unmanned Undersea vehicles (LDUUVs) that could potentially accomplish many of the missions now assigned to manned submarines. In this article, the authors address these issues and also discuss the tremendous potential UUVs have for future operators. They also provide plausible operational scenarios for consideration.

# "UNMANNED, UNSEEN, AND UNDER THE SEA"

By LCDR Brent Johnson, USN, and VADM John Richardson, USN,
U.S. Naval Institute *Proceedings* (June 2011): 42–47.

Like nuclear-powered submarines and submarine-launched ballistic missiles, unmanned undersea vehicles (UUVs) have the potential to radically change warfare below the surface. They can not only extend the reach of submarines, but also introduce new missions. This fresh potential requires us to closely examine, and where necessary change, the doctrine, tactics, techniques, and procedures we use to fully exploit this opportunity.

A well-thought-out experimentation plan will sharpen understanding of these rapidly developing systems. Through exploring, testing, and validating concepts of synergized platforms, sensors, and weapons, we will guide future payloads, payload volumes, and launchers into submarines and ships. At Commander Submarine Forces headquarters, the focus is on moving briskly to test not only the technology, but also the command and control architectures that will optimize future operations and warfighting. We want to be ready when more advanced systems come on line—and many of the technologies are already available.

Through conducting limited-scope experimentation with the existing generation of manned and unmanned systems, we can learn a tremendous amount about their capabilities and limitations. At the same time, we can gain insight into the command structures at sea and ashore needed to man, train, and equip a truly combined undersea force; even unmanned systems require maintenance, support, and in some cases remote operators. Learning about the communications and physical interfaces will enable us to launch, control, and recover these unmanned systems. It's an exciting time to be participating in the next step of undersea warfighting. UUVs can become invaluable force-multipliers, as the following fictional scenario illustrates.

## Caribbean Sea, 26 April 2021, 1035 Local Time

At the Joint Interagency Task Force–South headquarters in Key West, Florida, the watch team is riveted on the P-8 maritime patrol aircraft video feed. It has been a busy morning: A UUV conducting an intelligence, surveillance, and reconnaissance (ISR) mission near a small fishing village has made the first detection of a cocaine-laden mini-sub leaving the coast. These drug submarines, built in the deep jungle, have become increasingly sophisticated over time and are now the vehicle of choice for narco-trafficking. Often they net $75 million per trip between North America, Africa, and Europe.

The joint task force's large-diameter UUV (LDUUV) has sufficient range and speed to track the drug sub, but the team prefers to maintain it on station to continue collecting intelligence while planting and recovering more remote audio and video sensors. Informed by audio and video feed from the LDUUV and its network of remote sensors, and communicating through real-time chat with the area undersea warfare commander watch team in Norfolk, Virginia, the Joint Interagency Task Force–South shifts drug-sub tracking to the supporting P-8, while coordinating an interdiction with Coast Guard and other Navy assets.

The task-force commander then exercises previously delegated undersea domain authority (granted by the area undersea warfare commander) to extend assigned water space to the LDUUV at the port entry. The mini-sub, its crew, and illegal cargo will soon be in custody, while the LDUUV continues its covert mission. Several weeks later, Joint Interagency Task Force–South will release it from ISR tasking. The unmanned vehicle will depart its surveillance area and rendezvous with a transiting destroyer for recovery.

## Indian Ocean, 26 April 2021, 2235 Local Time

Halfway around the world, tensions have been escalating over the previous month and are nearly at the breaking point. A particularly troublesome coastal nation is flexing its muscles by announcing it will control shipping traffic through a major international strait. A U.S. carrier strike group is en route to the strait to back up U.S. diplomacy with military force. Captain Slade Cutter, the area undersea warfare commander battle-watch captain in Yokosuka, Japan, has the mission to support the Joint Force Maritime Component Commander as he works to maintain access to these critical sea lanes.

Captain Cutter reviews the assets available in the area: two undersea gliders, one ISR LDUUV, two subsea surveillance LDUUVs, and the USS *New Hampshire* (SSN-778). Because of the level of tensions and the anti-access area-denial threat to surface ships, no independent U.S. warships are present in the area—the inbound carrier strike group will be the first surface operations in the strait since tensions have begun escalating.

Oceanographic gliders have been patrolling the area for months, collecting hydrographic data and feeding a database of environmental conditions used to improve undersea sensing and weapon effectiveness. The *New Hampshire* is on patrol, armed with 12 Tomahawks, 16 ADCAP (advanced capability) torpedoes, and 8 long-range strike torpedoes. She is carrying an improved drydeck shelter capable of automated LDUUV launch and recovery.

The ISR LDUUV has been operating in theater since deployment by the departing USS *Forth Worth* (LCS-3) some 45 days ago. To extend its endurance, the *New Hampshire* has used her drydeck shelter to briefly recover the unmanned vehicle and recharge its batteries, download all of its intelligence data, and restock its payload dispensers with additional deployable sensors and communications nodes. Topped off with energy and payloads, the vehicle was redeployed three days ago in anticipation of another two months of on-station operations.

Two subsea surveillance LDUUVs were deployed 20 days ago from the USS *Coronado* (LCS-4), operating 400 miles off shore. Each was recharged by the *New Hampshire* and operates under the control of the *Coronado*, which processes their exfiltrated data and retasks the vehicles when necessary.

As the pace of developments picks up, Captain Cutter needs more continuous monitoring of the belligerent nation's submarines, which are still in port. He tasks the ISR LDUUV to lay a distributed acoustic and video array at the mouth of the adversary's major naval submarine port nearest the strait, and securely exfiltrate the data to the *New Hampshire*. The unmanned vehicle navigates to the harbor via GPS and bottom contours, and deploys its sensors and communications nodes. Captain Cutter knows this distributed sensor network will provide immediate indications of a hostile submarine heading for the strait and enable the *New Hampshire* to take appropriate action consistent with the rules of engagement. The American submarine assumes a covert posture just off the coast of the hostile nation, collecting data with her organic sensors, monitoring LDUUV collection highlights in real time, and remaining positioned to take action if necessary. The unmanned vehicle pushes data securely to the submarine by using a combination of high-frequency acoustic communications and semi-submerged relay nodes, enabling the *New Hampshire* to maintain her intelligence, surveillance, and reconnaissance posture closer to the strait while remaining aware of collections that the vehicle continues to make.

If further resolution is required, the SSN can launch a small unmanned aerial vehicle (UAV) on short notice to provide the continuous video feed required for positive target identification. On the area undersea warfare commander watch floor in Yokosuka, Captain Cutter has good situational awareness. The combination of manned and unmanned systems gives him an up-close picture of the tactical and operational environment. In addition, he has manned platforms in the theater that are connected to even more data and capable of taking the action dictated by the situation.

## Technology with Revolutionary Potential

These scenarios are not as futuristic as they may seem. We already have much of this technology. As is the case for many other military innovations, it is the creative combination of existing technologies that will be decisive. Secretary of the Navy Ray Mabus recently issued a series of unmanned systems goals, framing the Navy's investment strategy in this area for ground, air, surface, and subsurface systems for the next decade. The objective in the undersea domain is to "deploy large-diameter unmanned undersea vehicles (LDUUVs) from an operational UUV squadron, on independent missions, by 2020." In support of this vision, the Navy is moving to achieve two milestones by 2018:

- Commission a UUV squadron. This team will continue operational experimentation; develop tactics, techniques, and procedures; and begin mission planning.

- Achieve longer endurance and greater autonomy, building to a goal of fully autonomous operations for 70 days submerged.

Admiral Gary Roughead, Chief of Naval Operations, has been pressing for some time for advanced development and rapid fielding of unmanned systems. He has articulated a clear vision of the pivotal role that unmanned systems will play in the Navy's future force structure, and in 2008 he tasked the Strategic Studies Group to examine how unmanned systems will complement manned systems in the future. Under his direction, the Information Dominance Directorate has developed a detailed roadmap that supports the secretary's goals. Not only does this cover UUVs, it also includes fixed and mobile sensor networks like those employed in the scenarios presented here.

Fleet experimentation and limited real-world operations have demonstrated the potential of unmanned maritime systems to support force multiplication and mission accomplishment using fewer manned platforms. The secretary's ambitious—but achievable—goals highlight the Navy's commitment to expand the range of UUV capabilities and apply them in a wide variety of warfighting roles. The projected advances in these vehicles, distributed sensing systems, and communications will create opportunities limited only by our operational imagination.

## Working Far Forward Clandestinely

Identifying the command and control requirements for integrating UUVs and manned submarines will ultimately provide the framework for implementing many of these anticipated changes. As we define these command, control, and communications (C3) structures, however, we must remember that the fundamental role of undersea forces is to operate far forward in areas that are denied to other naval forces, exploiting concealment for their military effectiveness. Forward undersea operations within an adversary's anti-access and area-denial perimeter have emphasized limited communication transmissions, stealth, independent operations, and a high degree of operational autonomy.

The C3 structure for integrating manned and unmanned undersea platforms must align well with this kind of operational posture, as these same factors will continue to control the frequency, duration, and predictability of submarine and, ultimately, UUV communications. Advances in communications technology can at times bridge the gap, but determined adversaries will continue to develop detection and geo-location technology.

History provides many examples of undersea forces that were destroyed because they mistakenly believed their communications to be secure. Accordingly, it is important to identify some foundational principles that should guide our development of C3 structures for integrating undersea systems. To accomplish this, the following points need to be kept in mind.

- Manned undersea platforms should continue to be granted the greatest possible operational autonomy. For submarines, this means operational commanders must craft their Guidance and Intent statements in a way that allows commanding officers not only to understand the mission, but to exercise boldness and initiative, discriminately applying the capabilities of the sub and unmanned assets to seize fleeting opportunities to achieve mission goals.

- True receive-only communications methods must push information to forward undersea assets. No acknowledgement should be required unless militarily necessary.

- Transmissions from forward undersea platforms need to be minimized and conducted via expendable communications buoys or other unmanned systems whenever possible. Transmissions directly from stealthy manned platforms forward should also be minimized; when necessary, they must be sent via the least exploitable medium.

- Undersea systems can use short-range local communications to coordinate operations and share information whenever possible. Reach-back, long-haul communications should be used only when specifically necessary. For unmanned systems, the ability of UUVs and remote sensors to operate under the control of a manned submarine is particularly attractive in this context.

• We need to assume for the foreseeable future that unmanned systems will expend ordnance only under the specific direction of a human with some ability, to validate that a correct target is being engaged. This means unmanned systems with weapons will need a more robust C3 structure than unweaponized systems.

Some command and control issues are not unique to the undersea domain; they simply become more complex as the environment becomes more crowded. Just as the employment of widely varying unmanned aerial systems has complicated the task of controlling and coordinating air sorties, so the proliferation of UUVs that vary in size, range, payload, host platform, and mission area could make the job of undersea traffic control more challenging. This analogy suggests that an undersea tasking order similar to an air tasking order might become a necessary tool for coordinating and eventually optimizing undersea activity. Such an order would be a next logical step, building on the concepts of water-space management (preventing fratricide from undersea weapon employment) and prevention of mutual interference (undersea collisions). The undersea tasking order must go further, however, because it has to optimize the collective warfighting capability of forward undersea systems without unduly detracting from their autonomy.

Clearly, the full warfighting potential of manned and unmanned underwater systems working together requires overcoming numerous technological and conceptual challenges. The magnitude of these technological challenges in particular should not be understated. Our efforts to address the concepts, therefore, must be balanced with reasonable expectations about what is technologically feasible in the near term while remaining flexible enough to adapt to future developments. We will continue to use experimentation and fleet operations to evaluate and validate potential solutions that address the doctrinal and organizational issues raised by introduction of widespread unmanned vehicles.

## Indian Ocean, 28 April 2021, 1821 Local Time

The crisis in the strait has worsened considerably. The belligerent nation has stepped up its hostile rhetoric by threatening to attack any U.S. forces that attempt to intervene, a clear message directed at the inbound carrier strike group. Demonstrating its resolve, the enemy launches salvos of antiship missiles while the carrier strike group is still 200 miles from the strait. With these defeated, the strike group continues inbound.

But then the situation changes fundamentally. In 12 hours it will be morning, and the carrier strike group will be entering the strait. By then, Captain Cutter and his watch team must have taken decisive action to ensure security of the strike group from undersea threats. This necessity is substantiated by reports from multiple intelligence streams, including the ISR LDUUV, that one of the hostile submarines is preparing to get under way. It will be destroyed before exiting the harbor; it will not even be allowed to submerge. The *New Hampshire* is the best candidate to conduct such a surgical attack.

Captain Cutter exercises a "freeze" command to contain the LDUUV in a collapsed area. This immediately frees up water space for use by the American submarine and her weapons. From miles away, the *New Hampshire* launches two extended-range strike torpedoes that maneuver like undersea Tomahawks, following predetermined paths into the harbor and to the submarine piers.

Infrared imagery from a small UAV deployed by the *New Hampshire* enables the submarine to monitor the target while the strike torpedoes are inbound. If the enemy sub gets under way, one or both of the torpedoes can be shifted from strike mode to acoustic mode to complete the attack. The crew of the *New Hampshire* follows the progress of the torpedoes via data returned by the fiber-optic wire connection. After viewing the target image fed back by the weapon, they authorize it to complete its attack. The first weapon works flawlessly, breaking the enemy submarine in half at the pier, as confirmed by UAV real-time video battle-damage assessment. The second is diverted to its secondary target, a floating drydock with another enemy submarine.

Captain Cutter releases the ISR LDUUV from its freeze condition. In the strait, the subsea surveillance unmanned underwater vehicles confirm there are no changes on the seabed that might indicate the presence of mines. With both the submarine and mine threats eliminated, the carrier strike group is able to enter the strait unmolested by threats below the surface.

As this scenario shows, future naval operations and maritime security will include an increasing mix of unmanned systems, and the need to effectively coordinate their operations will become even more important and challenging. UUVs will introduce revolutionary capabilities, but their full potential will be achieved only if their command and control provides for successful integration with manned platforms. The concepts and supporting principles presented here aim to accomplish this level of integration while at the same time allowing undersea forces to operate autonomously, preserving their greatest asymmetric capability of stealth.

With UUV technical development moving forward, we must use these guiding principles to ensure that doctrinal and organizational arrangements, as well as C3 structures, allow the revolutionary potential of UUVs to be realized so that they become true force multipliers.

# PART III

## CYBER, the Most Disruptive Technology

# 13 "THE NAVY'S NEWEST WARFIGHTING IMPERATIVE"

VADM Kendall L. Card, USN, and VADM Michael S. Rogers, USN

In the third part of this **Wheel Book** we focus on what may very well be the most disruptive technology of the past fifty years: the computer. In modern lexicon, the term "cyber" is used as a prefix that means "computer" or "computer network," as in *cyberspace,* the electronic medium in which online communication takes place. Many observers contend that the opening shots of the next war will likely occur in cyberspace. In this article, the authors present a reasoned argument that the United States must be dominant in the information domain, and they discuss how the Navy is working to achieve this goal. This discussion provides a firm foundation for understanding the countless stories about "computer hacking" that fill the evening news.

## "THE NAVY'S NEWEST WARFIGHTING IMPERATIVE"

By VADM Kendall L. Card, USN, and VADM Michael S. Rogers, USN, U.S. Naval Institute *Proceedings* (October 2012): 22–26.

In the maritime operating environment, enormous challenges have been created by the explosive growth and global pervasiveness of information technology, its relatively low cost compared with that of conventional warfare systems, and the ease with which it can be "weaponized" to degrade or deny the U.S. Navy's overwhelming superiority. Moreover, those hostile to the United States incessantly exploit our networks, necessitating our constant vigilance and aggressive, intelligent action.

These everyday realities, combined with information's prominence in national, joint, coalition, and Navy strategic objectives, have compelled us to organize and use the Navy's information "portfolio" in a way that achieves real warfighting capability. The January 2012 guidance *Sustaining U.S. Leadership: Priorities for 21st Century Defense, the 2012 Chairman's Strategic Direction for the Joint Force,* and the *Chief of Naval Operations' Sailing Directions and Navigation Plan* are all replete with objectives consistent with this. Just as the United States dominates the maritime domain, we must do the same in the information realm, which includes cyberspace and the electromagnetic spectrum, if we are to preserve our Navy's superiority and primacy.

From our perspective, this is a new center of gravity for maritime warfare. Optimizing information is critical to the Navy's core capabilities of forward presence, deterrence, sea control, power projection, maritime security, humanitarian assistance, and disaster response. Controlling the information domain, therefore, is a warfighting imperative that must be mainstreamed into the Navy as an operational discipline alongside air, surface, and submarine warfare.

## Contextualizing Information Dominance

At some level, most Navy personnel understand the importance of information to the service's mission. However, to appreciate its dominance as a warfighting discipline, it is necessary to view it in a broader context, one that characterizes and clarifies its essential forms in warfare and as warfare. Each of these representations influences the way the Navy organizes, resources, and executes its missions. Although each category presents a warfighting risk, there is also tremendous opportunity as we defend our asymmetric capability presented by these technologies. We must learn to consider information in any or all of the following ways, according to the situation and overall context:

*Enabler:* Access to superior information has been a military essential for millennia, but the importance of acquiring, exploiting, protecting, and moving combat information has become increasingly critical. What has changed is the instantaneous speed and massive volume at which it can be discovered, accessed, processed, exploited, and disseminated, regardless of its origin or intended destination. Enabled by these technologies, the military force that senses, processes, and delivers information more efficiently and effectively than its adversary will enjoy enhanced and predictive battlespace awareness, better command and control (C2), and greater decisional agility.

*Weapon:* The Navy is inextricably dependent on cyberspace and its information and networks, along with the terrestrial and space transport paths for its operations. In effect, the network and its components (information, intelligence, technology, people) have become a combat system. In this form, the network can serve as a platform from which to launch information as a weapon. As an enabler (information in warfare), it has evolved as a nonkinetic weapon (information as warfare). As noted previously, the military force that best uses its networks and cyberspace to exploit and attack the vulnerabilities of its adversaries will have a combat advantage. Moreover, the integration of nonkinetic or electromagnetic strike options with traditional kinetic fires will significantly enhance the overall warfighting effect. This is why the network must be operated and "fought" as a warfare platform, in the same way as are aircraft, ships, and submarines.

*Threat:* Connectivity provides Navy platforms and weapon systems with unprecedented speed, agility, and precision. It also opens numerous attack vectors for adept cyber opponents. Cyberspace has a relatively low barrier of entry for adversaries to effectively challenge and hold Navy forces at risk. Over the past several years, states, terrorist organizations, "hacktivist" groups, organized criminals, and individual hackers have attempted to exploit Navy networks. These efforts have served to map and exploit seams in our networks, facilitate massive information theft, deny and degrade our access to cyberspace, undermine confidence in the integrity of our data, and disrupt our C2, combat systems, and dependence on over-the-horizon intelligence. The threats, combined with the worldwide proliferation of advanced long-range weapon systems and opponents' cyberspace capabilities, have the potential to reduce the Navy's technological and operational advantage.

*Warfare domain:* As detailed here, warfare's historical domains have been physical, and platforms—infantry, cavalry, tanks, ships, submarines, aircraft, and spacecraft—have served in both supporting capacities (enabling combat) and supported roles (engaging in combat). The relevance of the physical domains and their associated platforms has remained largely unchanged, but what is new, with the advent of radio, computer, and network technology, is the emergence of the electromagnetic spectrum—specifically cyberspace—as not only an enabler of the physical domains and their respective platforms, but as a warfighting domain in its own right. The network and the electromagnetic spectrum are fundamentally the battlespace within this realm. They are likely to figure largely in future conflicts and crises, and the military force that most effectively engages in cyberspace will create an advantage.

## Operational Constructs

Within this context, we define information dominance as the operational advantage gained from fully integrating the Navy's information functions, capabilities, and resources in a way that optimizes decision making and maximizes warfighting effects. It includes cyber, intelligence, surveillance, reconnaissance, networks, communications, space, meteorology, oceanography, electronic warfare, and of course the electromagnetic spectrum. It also encompasses the constituent components (resources, capabilities, governance, tactics, techniques, procedures) that must be marshaled and aligned with doctrine, organization, training, materiel, logistics, personnel, and facilities.

Our vision for information dominance is assured maritime C2 and superior battlespace awareness that allow for sustained, integrated fires across the full range of maritime warfare. These three fundamental facets will posture the Navy to maneuver and engage its opponents at the nexus of the maritime and information domains. When all three are achieved, they provide Navy commanders with the ability to operate freely in the information domain, well ahead of the adversary's decision cycle.

*Assured C2:* The Navy must ensure its ability to command and control forces. This requires capabilities that permit commanders to exchange orders with subordinates, target and conduct strikes as part of the joint force, and assess the results. Navy mission success—from sensing the environment to understanding our opponents to operating and defending our communications and linked systems—is inextricably linked to the assurance of C2.

*Battlespace awareness:* This is the traditional mission of the constituent components of meteorology, oceanography, intelligence, cryptology, communications, networks, space, and electronic warfare. It leverages persistent surveillance of the maritime and information battlespace, penetrating knowledge of the abilities and intent of our adversaries. It provides an understanding of when, where, and how they operate, and of their expertise within the electromagnetic spectrum. When performed in harmony, these skills and knowledge provide the target acquisition and targeting solutions necessary to execute successful strikes.

*Integrated fires:* With information dominance the Navy can use its networks, cyberspace, and space to exploit and attack the vulnerabilities of its antagonists to achieve nonkinetic effects (i.e., fires). This proficiency maximizes the Navy's dominance of the electromagnetic spectrum to deny its use by potential enemies for their own operations. Nonkinetic attacks may augment and provide an alternative to kinetic weapons, thus satisfying a commander's combat objective with stealth and less or no physical destruction. Therefore, the ability to integrate these types of strike options with traditional kinetic fires multiplies the warfighting advantage.

## The Cyberspace Dimension

Cyberspace is the digital "fabric" that weaves into the information environment individual, organizational, corporate, government, and military entities. It is elemental to their operations and permeates the physical domains. The Navy leverages cyberspace to provide commanders with operational and tactical advantages. Practically all major systems on ships, aircraft, submarines, and unmanned vehicles are networked to some degree. This includes most combat, communications, engineering, and position, navigation, and timing systems. Additionally, cyberspace extends equally across joint and Navy business and industrial control systems.

Allowing for speed, agility, and precision in a broad range of missions, cyberspace delivers the reliable, secure communications that are essential to effective C2. Network-centric weapon systems like the Tactical Tomahawk use cyberspace to receive in-flight targeting data from operational command centers. Similarly, carrier aviation maintenance programs rely on it to deliver mission-ready aircraft. Even the most routine activities, such as training, education, medical, and logistical functions are conducted via cyberspace. Despite its speed and convenience, however, it is laden with vulnerabilities and threats that can affect Navy networks and reduce combat readiness.

Because of the service's increased reliance on these types of operations, cyberspace superiority and our maritime dominance are essentially interdependent. Success in the maritime domain and joint operational environment depends in no small part on our ability to maintain freedom of maneuver-and-deliver effects in cyberspace. Therefore, protecting access to it is just as paramount as is protecting sea lines of communications. This is why, in addition to the previously listed fundamental facets of information dominance, the Navy:

- Operates, defends, exploits, and engages in cyberspace to ensure access for all mission-critical functions and to provide Navy and joint commanders with resilient C2 capabilities. This is assured access to cyberspace and confident C2.

- Evaluates adversary actions in cyberspace through dedicated cyber-intelligence collection and analysis, and by fully integrating timely and relevant cyber information and threat warnings into the commander's operational picture. These measures are intended to prevent strategic surprise in cyberspace.

- Delivers decisive cyber effects at a time and place of the operational commander's choosing, across the full range of military operations in support of the commanders' objectives.

## From Abstract to Reality

The Navy has laid the organizational foundation for dominating cyberspace and the electromagnetic spectrum by consolidating the resources and manpower for its information-intensive programs, commissioning the U.S. Fleet Cyber Command to serve as its component commander to U.S. Cyber Command, and establishing Navy Cyber Forces as the type commander for these important mission areas.

To further enhance the service's use of information in warfare, we will concentrate changes and improvements in three core areas: warfare development, warfighter development, and warfighting capability. We will produce and employ new operating concepts and a Fleet-level concept of operations and tactics, techniques, and procedures. We will also improve our recruiting, selecting, educating, and training of information-related professionals. Finally, future warfare capabilities will focus on better controlling the electromagnetic spectrum, extending our defensive and offensive capabilities in the cyberspace domain, and maintaining the speed, agility, and adaptability of our decision-making and C2 abilities during operations in a communication-degraded or -denied environment. Ultimately, these efforts will yield the following, which will result in information dominance as a warfighting discipline:

- Secure C2
- Persistent, predictive battlespace awareness
- Unified combat information
- Integrated kinetic and nonkinetic fires
- Technology innovation
- An optimized information workforce
- Reforms in planning, programming, budgeting, execution, and acquisition

## The Future Is Now

While the Navy is making increasing use of all forms of information for peacetime and wartime operations, the relevance of information dominance has never been greater, particularly as our adversaries design new ways to exploit our networks and inhibit our mastery of the electromagnetic spectrum. Of equal concern is the expanding number of critical shipboard and airborne systems, including combat, communications, engineering, and positioning, navigation, and timing systems that are linked and vulnerable to cyber attack. A more holistic view of what constitutes "the network" is required—across type commands, systems commands, resource sponsors, operational users, and security classifications—to ensure that interoperability and defensive measures are built in and actively employed.

Lastly, the cold, hard reality of increasingly constrained budgets in the immediate future forces us to make tough programmatic and fiscal choices that will doubtless limit the scope and range of enhancements the Navy must have to rule the information domain. Nevertheless, we continue to organize, train, and resource a credible workforce, developing forward-leaning, interoperable, and resilient information capabilities.

In spite of the challenges we face in achieving assured C2, battlespace awareness, and integrated fires, the future has arrived, and there is no turning back. Information in all its forms will continue to evolve. We must evolve with it. Whether characterized as cyber, intelligence, surveillance, reconnaissance, networks, communications, space, meteorology, oceanography, or electronic warfare, this new center of gravity in maritime warfare means that information dominance has become a Navy warfighting imperative.

# 14 "A NEW ERA IN NAVAL WARFARE"

VADM Ted M. Branch, USN

**In this article, the author discusses** the Navy's efforts to reorganize itself to deal with the disruptive technologies that could potentially lead to cyber-conflict. Speaking from his vantage point as the Deputy Chief of Naval Operations for Information Dominance (N2/N6) Vice Admiral Branch explains the concept of information dominance as a warfighting capability and details the three pillars of the concept: assured command and control, battlespace awareness, and integrated fires. He also discusses the roles and missions of the recently formed Information Dominance Corps within the U.S. Navy.

## "A NEW ERA IN NAVAL WARFARE"

By VADM Ted M. Branch, USN, U.S. Naval Institute *Proceedings*
(July 2014): 18–22.

Our Navy's forward presence protects the interconnected global system of trade and reinforces the security of the U.S. economy. Our engagement around the world reassures allies, builds trust with partners and friends, and prevents and deters wars. We are the foundation of the nation's "away game," endowed with operational agility, possessed with innovative resourcefulness, and armed with credible combat power to be used where it matters, when it matters. Sustaining our global primacy requires that we dominate the battlespace on, above, and below the surface of the sea, as well as outer space. However, successfully commanding, controlling, and fighting our forces in these areas requires dominance in the information domain, to include the electromagnetic spectrum and cyberspace.

The name we've given to this concept—information dominance—is still new and unfamiliar to some, but it's indispensable to Fleet operations, so much so that we've adopted it as a distinct warfare discipline. Formerly perceived by many as a collection of support activities performed by specialized restricted line officers, information dominance is increasingly recognized by Fleet operators as a critical force multiplier. It's no longer just an adjunct to warfighting. It is warfighting.

## Alpha and Omega

Imagine a hypothetical scenario in which U.S. naval forces respond when the country of Omega, long envious of Alpha's energy resources, attempts to overrun Alpha's defenses and seize its oil fields. Due to our array of unmanned systems, multi-intelligence sensor and processing capacity, and robust cyber capabilities, the U.S. fleet detects Omega's intentions early and quickly succeeds in attaining dominance of the information battlespace without Omega's knowledge.

Leveraging operational surprise through mastery of the electromagnetic spectrum (EMS), the U.S. forces arrive on station before Omega can launch its initial assault into Alpha. The U.S. commander is equipped with a penetrating knowledge of Omega's force disposition, intentions, capabilities, and vulnerabilities. Our fleet's unexpected arrival causes Omega to pause momentarily, providing time for U.S. forces to finalize their preparation of the battlespace and conduct offensive operations in cyberspace and the EMS.

U.S. oceanographers possess unmatched knowledge of the physical battlespace, including expected weather conditions, currents, sea-states, and tides. The U.S. commander knows where Omega's assets are likely to operate and when and where they cannot operate. This insight allows the U.S. commander to position his or her forces and deploy intelligence, surveillance, and reconnaissance (ISR) resources. He also knows the effect of the physical environment on propagation and ducting, enabling the U.S. Fleet's Information Technology and Information Warfare professionals to tailor the friendly communications posture and electronic-warfare support measures most effectively. The U.S. commander sees the EMS from Omega's perspective, as well as his own, allowing the luxury of maneuvering freely and rapidly through the spectrum and take offensive actions to Omega's disadvantage.

U.S. intelligence capability has given our forces keen insight into Omega leadership's mission objectives, intent, C4ISR systems, and fine-grain targeting data on Omega's submarines, minefields, and missile launchers. This allows the U.S. fleet to evade detection and targeting during the critical early stages of the confrontation. Similarly, our knowledge of Omega network capabilities and force disposition allows us to implement preplanned responses that negate and defeat Omega's offensive efforts in cyberspace.

Through a combination of kinetic strikes and network degradation, U.S. forces are able to diminish Omega's command and control and destroy its limited maritime-patrol/over-the-horizon targeting assets, as well as its antiship ballistic- and cruise-missile capability. As a consequence, the confidence of Omega's leadership is shaken by a lack of situational awareness, degraded command and control over its forces, and distrust of its sensors and warfighting capabilities, especially its non-kinetic assets. At this point, the Omega commander is overwhelmingly disadvantaged, unable to execute the planned invasion of Alpha, or strike a symbolic blow against the U.S. Fleet.

This obviously simplified scenario illuminates the operations that information dominance delivers.

## What It Is

Our formal definition of information dominance is the operational advantage gained from fully integrating the Navy's information functions, capabilities, and resources to optimize decision making and maximize warfighting effects. In other words, it means delivering decision-quality information where it matters and when it matters. It fosters freedom of maneuver in all domains, and integrates our fires, which may be projected through the network (or cyberspace or the electromagnetic spectrum) for soft kill, or delivered through the physical environment for hard kill. To make these capabilities possible, we will master the information domain, just as we've mastered the air, surface, undersea, and space domains. Accordingly, information dominance focuses on:

- Robust and agile command and control (C2) in all operating environments
- Superior knowledge of the battlespace, both the physical environment as well as threat capability, disposition, and intent
- Projecting power through the integration of kinetic and non-kinetic effects

We refer to these three elements, or pillars, as assured C2, battlespace awareness, and integrated fires. Through them, information dominance creates decision superiority, provides asymmetric advantage, and enhances the lethality of our deployed forces with non-kinetic options. By design, the pillars correspond to the Chief of Naval Operations' three tenets:

*Warfighting First:* With assured C2 and enhanced battlespace awareness, commanders are able to definitively assess threats and determine their most efficient and effective courses of action using the range of kinetic weapons and non-kinetic effects available to them.

*Operate Forward:* Ensuring freedom of maneuver in cyberspace and the EM spectrum, and assuring the ability to direct operations and coordinate actions in contested environments is paramount for successful operations forward. Our evolving ISR assets combined with our established meteorology and oceanography capabilities contribute to battlespace awareness by delivering information on the threat and physical environments, ensuring effective Fleet operations. Reliable connectivity to the global information grid allows us to operate forward. What's more, the global disposition of our forces contributes essential information (e.g., intelligence, weather, etc.) for dissemination to forces forward.

*Be Ready:* Maintaining a continuously refreshed awareness of the operating environment, including threat capabilities and intentions, allows us to be predictive, enabling our ability to prepare and coordinate well in advance of forward operations.

The critical element of the information dominance definition is *integration.* Blending the attributes of intelligence, surveillance, reconnaissance, oceanography, meteorology, networks, cyber, electronic warfare (EW), etc. allows for better planning, smarter decisions, and earlier results. Aligning the related restricted-line communities of Naval Oceanography, Information Warfare, Information Professional, Intelligence, and the Space Cadre into the Information Dominance Corps has likewise advanced our concept and capability development, and improved data and system interoperability. To borrow a cliché, in the case of Navy information dominance the whole is much greater than the sum of its parts. Comprehending it, however, requires a slightly deeper dive into the three pillars.

## Assured Command and Control

Assured C2 makes the issuing of orders to distributed forces and the coordination of maneuver and fires across the warfighting domains (air, land, sea, space, cyberspace, and the EMS) possible. It provides the ability to monitor the status of our forces and assess the effectiveness of our fires. It is indispensable to forward operations and securely networks our forces in all threat environments.

Practically every major system in the Fleet is "networked" to some degree, including most combat, communications, engineering, and position, navigation, and timing capabilities. Cyberspace extends that network across joint and Navy business and industrial-control systems. While this connectivity provides unprecedented speed, agility, and precision, it also opens attack vectors for determined adversaries. Therefore, assuring our C2 requires a robust, protected, resilient, and reliable information infrastructure afloat, ashore, and overseas.

Maintaining a *protected transport* infrastructure securely links our forces ashore and afloat in permissive, contested, and denied C2 environments. Another key component is *resilient networks* that withstand the barrage of attacks we see today and expect to grow. We are increasing the integration and interoperability of the sea and shore segments of our enterprise architecture through technologies such as cloud computing. Moreover, we are aligning with the DOD's Joint Information environment and the Intelligence community's Information-Technology enterprise frameworks to enhance interoperability and expand our ability to share and receive information from joint and national partners. Assured Positioning, Navigation, and Timing (PNT) provides for the safety of navigation, targeting, and C2 across our platforms and systems.

In his seminal 2012 *Proceedings* article "Imminent Domain," Chief of Naval Operations Admiral Jonathan Greenert observed that "[a] culture of electromagnetic silencing and understanding of electronic signatures will have to permeate our efforts if we are to command the EM-cyber environment." Toward the objective of mastering the EM environment, the emerging Real-Time Spectrum-Operations system will allow us to monitor the spectrum continuously, identify conflicts, determine solutions, and differentiate between unintentional interference and intentional jamming. As current prototypes evolve, we'll leverage this knowledge to create effects and "hide in plain sight."

In a nutshell, the assured C2 pillar touches almost everything we do, afloat and ashore. It complements the battlespace awareness and integrated fires pillars and provides the communications we require in the most demanding conditions. We are progressing down this path with our Next-Generation enterprise network, Consolidated Afloat network enterprise system, Automated Digital network system, and Navy Multiband Terminal programs.

## Battlespace Awareness

This is knowledge of the operating environment that allows the warfighter to find, penetrate, and predict the enemy's operations by making better decisions faster. It gives us home-field advantage at the away games. It requires a superior understanding of the battlespace, to include the physical environment, cyber-space, the EM spectrum, and the threat. It also requires immediate and con-tinuous access to essential information that updates the operational picture, facilitating prediction and decisive action. The warfighting advantage created by battlespace awareness comprises functions and payloads that are interoper-able and capable of rapid upgrade relative to the threat. Battlespace awareness capabilities therefore require advanced means to sense, collect, process, exploit, and disseminate information in real time.

In the case of *sensing* and *collecting*, we leverage manned and unmanned, fixed, mobile, and distributed systems, and we coordinate across the force through a seamless communication architecture. Our manned capabilities include the EP-3 aircraft, surveillance towed-array vessels, and fixed surveillance systems. Unmanned systems, such as our MQ-4C Triton Unmanned Aircraft System, MQ-8B/C Fire Scout Vertical Takeoff Unmanned Aerial Vehicle, and Unmanned Carrier-Launched Airborne Surveillance and Strike System, are key components because of their persistence and the reduced risk to our manned platforms and crews. Their increasing numbers and missions ultimately give us more options and greater operational flexibility. By stressing payloads over platforms, we are able to quickly leverage standard interfaces and common control systems, which also permit rapid technology upgrades, allowing us to pace the threat.

In *processing, exploiting,* and *disseminating,* our path to superior decisions starts with ensuring that data derived from our own sensors, as well as from joint and national sources, are delivered to deployed commanders when needed. This requires sophisticated tools that pull multiple sources of data with common standards into a single picture, process high volumes of information, and save thousands of man hours both afloat and ashore at Maritime Operations Cen-ters (MOC), Maritime Intelligence Operations Centers, the Naval Oceano-graphic Office, and the Office of Naval Intelligence, among others.

To further develop battlespace awareness, we are expanding the Pacific Fleet's Intelligence Federation model Navy-wide. The federation optimizes intel-ligence manning, collection, and communication assets. It will leverage the full range of information dominance capabilities, supplementing Navy regional expertise with the capabilities and assets of the combatant commands, combat support agencies, the intelligence community, and our allied partners. As these initiatives mature, we see the MOC becoming the essential platform for sustained battlespace awareness.

With a long-term focus on a critical physical aspect of battlespace awareness and emphasis on the Arctic, the Oceanographer of the Navy, Rear Admiral Jonathan White, led the recent update of the Navy Arctic Roadmap to ensure our readiness for potential contingencies in the polar north. Similarly, Rear Admiral White's office is preparing for the future effects of climate change, conducting vulnerability assessments of Navy coastal infrastructure and supporting DOD strategic planning with respect to potential impacts on the global security environment.

## Integrated Fires

This is the ability to project power across the kill chain. It blends non-kinetic effects with traditional kinetic weapons in order to fully exploit and, when necessary, attack adversary vulnerabilities. To be successful, it requires two mutually supporting functions:

- Disrupting/Denying/Defeating Red Fires. That is, preventing the adversary from initiating kinetic and non-kinetic operations of his own by disrupting his C4ISR and targeting ability.
- Enhancing Blue Fires, which requires dynamic collaboration across missions, domains, and with other services. This coordination permits the exploitation of the EMS as a weapon and the integration of targeting and fire-control capabilities for increased weapon range, effectiveness, and lethality. It includes the evolving electronic-warfare and offensive cyber weapons that complement our air, surface, and subsurface kinetic weapons.

We are making major investments in the Fleet's ability to maneuver freely and fight in the EM environment. Central to this investment is the concept of

EM Maneuver Warfare or EMW, which anticipates future conflicts in the battlespace created where cyber and the EM spectrum converge. Core to EMW is a complete awareness of our EM signature and others' in real time; the ability to manipulate our EM signature to control what others can detect, maximize our ability to defeat jamming and deception, and guarantee our use of the spectrum when needed; and use of EM and cyber capabilities as non-kinetic fires to inhibit adversary C4ISR, targeting, and combat capabilities. Successful EMW requires the seamless integration of the communications, command-and-control, signals intelligence, spectrum management, electronic warfare, and cyberspace disciplines to permit our freedom of action across the spectrum.

## The Information Dominance Corps

The 2010 consolidation of the OCEANO, Information Warfare, Information Professional, Intelligence, and Space Cadre officer communities—together with their enlisted, reserve, and civilian counterparts—established a professional and technically diverse corps that is rapidly coalescing into a formidable warfighting force. They aren't the only sailors executing information dominance as a warfare discipline, but they are its principal practitioners, and they bring extremely valuable skills and specialized knowledge to the fight. Moreover, they are taking on leadership roles at the highest levels, as exemplified most recently by Admiral Mike Rogers' confirmation as Commander, U.S. Cyber Command, and Director, National Security Agency/Central Security Service; as well as Vice Admiral Jan Tighe's command of Fleet Cyber Command/U.S. 10th Fleet.

Considering the exponential rate of change in technology and its corresponding impact on both our own and our adversaries' capabilities, the unique talents and abilities within the Information Dominance Corps are increasingly critical. While we have made concerted efforts to protect and strengthen the IDC's deep technical expertise in its traditional skill areas, we are mindful that broadening the experience of our members yields more capable information-dominance leaders. As a consequence, we're inserting common core training relevant to the broader information-dominance mission at set points in the IDC career path. Beginning with accessions and again at mid-career and senior points, we are bringing IDC members together with their peers to expand their interdisciplinary knowledge, build personal relationships, and engender an esprit de corps unique to this mission. Additionally, we're actively managing career paths and cross-detailing IDC leaders to broaden their experience and perspective. This mostly involves commissioned officers now, but will include senior enlisted and civilians as we define the process. The intended effect is a deliberate transformation of the IDC from a multidisciplinary group to a fully functional inter-disciplinary corps.

Information dominance is much bigger than the IDC, but the corps' leaders are the ones who understand it best. They are fully integrated with the Fleet and are gaining recognition as warfighters in their own right. From its beginnings in 2010, the corps has quickly matured, aggressively adapting to its warfighting mission. It has greater operational relevance and more warfighting credibility than ever before. Most important, IDC members are increasingly accepted as legitimate warfighters by traditional operators.

## The Information Dominance Type Command

Finally, we are establishing Navy Information Dominance Forces, an integrated type command dedicated to the discipline. With an initial operational capability of 1 October 2014, this new type command will subsume the existing Navy Cyber Forces command and integrate many of the man, train, and equip elements of Fleet Cyber Command, the Office of Naval Intelligence, and the Navy Oceanography and Meteorology Command. It will initially be led by a two-star IDC flag officer who will report to the Commander, U.S. Fleet Forces Command, right alongside the existing platform type commands.

The establishment of this command is another step in information dominance's maturation since its 2010 birth. It's the logical next phase in the discipline's evolution and, as we know from our experience with the platform type commands, it's consistent with the Navy's time-tested approach to institutionalizing other warfare areas. As it did with the advent of naval aviation, submarines, and nuclear power, the Navy is adapting to the technology of the age and maintaining its warfighting advantage.

The type command will integrate the man, train, and equip aspects of information dominance across the Fleet, coordinating closely with the platform type commands, the numbered fleets, systems commands, and strike groups to ensure information dominance is fully considered throughout the readiness kill chain. Given the network's universality within the larger shore-based Navy, the type command will eventually extend its man, train, and equip reach beyond the Fleet to facilitate information dominance readiness Navy-wide. It's an enormous undertaking—one that we must embrace with vigor.

Information dominance is a reality. Senior leaders across the Navy, including the CNO as well as Admirals William Gortney and Harry Harris, consider it essential to our sustained forward presence, credible combat power, and global influence. We are at the dawn of a new era in naval warfare, and information dominance is central to our continued prominence in an increasingly asymmetric and dangerous world. It is the way of the future for Information Age warfare.

# 15 "CREATING CYBER WARRIORS"

VADM Nancy Brown, USN; CAPT Danelle Barrett, USN;
and LCDR Jesse Castillo, USN

When people first encounter the term "cyber warriors" they often picture the fearsome robotic/cybernetic warriors from the popular *Terminator* science fiction films. In reality, the Navy's "cyber warriors" are more comfortable in dress blue uniforms than in titanium exoskeletons. In this article, the authors summarize the steps taken since 2009 to create and sustain the Information Dominance Corps (IDC). This community includes unrestricted line officers, enlisted personnel, and civilian experts in such diverse fields as computer network operations, meteorology/oceanography, signals intelligence, knowledge management, and other fields. Collectively, they are expected to be "forward-thinking, adaptive planners with superb technical skills, ideally suited to achieve advantages in a disruptive, rapidly changing battle space."

## "CREATING CYBER WARRIORS"

By VADM Nancy Brown, USN; CAPT Danelle Barrett, USN; and LCDR Jesse Castillo, USN, U.S. Naval Institute *Proceedings* (October 2012): 28–32.

In his 1 March 2012 opening remarks to the House of Committee on Appropriations, Defense Subcommittee, Chief of Naval Operations Admiral Jonathan W.

Greenert addressed the tenets that have guided his decisions as a naval officer. In particular, "Warfighting First means the Navy must be ready to fight and win today, while building the ability to win tomorrow." In 2009 the Navy took the very bold and forward-looking move to create the Information Dominance Corps (IDC), bringing together experts from the Navy's key information-related fields. This initiative realigned the intelligence, information-warfare (IW), meteorology/oceanography, information professional (IP), and cyber-warfare engineers into one restricted-line cadre of officers. After three years, it is time to ask ourselves if this construct has accomplished its stated purpose and whether it provides the properly skilled individuals to achieve the CNO's tenet of being able to win tomorrow. We believe this was an important first step, but the transformation must continue if we are to build and sustain a credible cyber capability.

Rather than artificially separating communities, we need to combine the right skills and talents into an unrestricted line community to produce the effects required to dominate in the cyber realm, the preeminent operational platform of the future. Restructuring to achieve this desirable blend of talent is necessary to meet the CNO's Sailing Directions objective to "provide superior awareness and control when and where we need it." Each of the current communities contributes valuable skills but only delivers a piece of what the aggregate requires and does not supply capability in the most effective, integrated manner for successful operations. Changes are needed to ensure we have an officer and enlisted corps aligned properly on all operational platforms and trained to meet future challenges.

## The New Officer

How will an officer community evolve to revolutionize modern warfare and affect traditional warfighting lines of operation? In today's era of technology-dependent actions, the professionals charged with functioning in the cyber domain must be trained to meet tomorrow's threats. This domain includes the physical operational platform for information, from the end user's computer through the network, radio frequency, space and unmanned- and autonomous-system transport pieces, to the information provider. It includes how that information is secured, organized, presented, and used for rapid and accurate decision making. To build the kind of force necessary to excel in the cybersphere, the Navy's entire man, train, and equip paradigm must be revamped to produce a new kind of officer equipped for the task: a cyber-warfare officer.

Dominating in the cyber realm requires investing in the right set of skills. The community charged with this task must be cultivated like others in the Navy operating in more traditional warfighting contexts. It must have an accession plan that recruits the right talent and brings them in as ensigns. These officers would become proficient through multiple tours, expanding in operational scope and technical breadth. On par with existing warfighting communities, the cyber-warfare community would be part of the unrestricted line. To do less only pays lip service to the importance of cyber operations and the significant, revolutionary role they will play in any future conflict.

The cyber-warfighting domain changes at an unprecedented pace. Technological breakthroughs can be achieved in hours rather than years. The cost of entry into cyber operations for the adversary is minuscule and the technology used is ubiquitous. Our forces can be quickly outstripped of any technological operational advantage if we are not agile and predictive in addressing potential threats and capabilities from an integrated, holistic, total-warfighting perspective. Events are measured in milliseconds and a response is required in an even shorter time.

Demand for cyber-warfare skills is increasing, and competition for the limited talent pool of true experts and visionaries is intense. Industry is recruiting college graduates with these skills at a rate far outpacing supply—a trend that is expected to continue. All of these factors support the need for a dedicated, experienced, and well-trained cadre of professionals, from ensign to admiral, to combat present and future threats. This is not an area where a pick-up team can be successful. We must be able to attract and retain the right talent to be a formidable force.

## The Right Mix

Having the right talent is the first step, and properly focusing that talent is the second. The set of core competencies the cyber community should focus on combines some traditional skills with those that are emerging and will be refined as the Navy's mission in the cyber domain evolves. Agility is key, and developing adaptive thinkers is critical. Initially, ensuring expertise in the following competencies is essential for a credible cyber force:

- Computer network operations, including both the attack and defend aspects
- Signals intelligence, radio frequency communications, and combat systems
- Influence operations and knowledge management
- Unmanned and autonomous systems.

Computer network operations consist of computer network attack, defense, and exploitation. According to Joint Doctrine for Information Operations (Joint Pub 3–13), these functions are defined as:

- Computer network attack: Actions taken through computer networks to disrupt, deny, degrade, or destroy the information in computers and computer networks or the computers and networks themselves.
- Computer network defense: Actions taken through such networks to protect, monitor, analyze, detect, and respond to network attacks, intrusions, disruptions, or other unauthorized actions that would compromise or cripple defense information systems and networks. Joint Publication 6.0 (Joint Communications System) further outlines computer network defense as an aspect of network operations.
- Computer network exploitation: Enabling actions and intelligence collection via computer networks that exploit data gathered from target or enemy information systems or networks.

Traditionally, these functions and the skills to support them have been divided among different communities. But this artificial separation is based on the legacy-community structures and missions, and it is the problem with the way cyber operations function today. In the case of network operations, the best defenders and service providers are those who know how to exploit and attack a network's potential vulnerabilities and understand the risks. The same group of officers needs expertise in all these areas.

Many similar fundamental skills are required to perform signals intelligence (communications and electronic intelligence) and to manage communications, combat systems, and the frequency spectrum. Knowledge of engineering and technology (for example, knowing how a signal or protocol was designed to work, understanding the relationship between signals and atmospherics, or how radio-frequency communications and systems operate) are key. Someone who understands all elements of the equation is much better poised to maximize friendly availability to these systems and deny the enemy use of their own.

On the combat-systems front, these assets are networked, and many also use their own signals and distinct portions of the frequency spectrum. Much of the same knowledge that the cyber-warfare officer needs to perform network operations, such as signals intelligence and spectrum management, would be employed for effective management of combat systems. This would also provide a solid basis for understanding enemy combat-systems capabilities and limitations. An officer with this background would be an indispensable member of any operational planning or targeting team.

## Influence Operations and Knowledge Management

"Influence operations" includes elements of traditional psychological operations combined with strategic communication and knowledge management to apply information for operational advantages. The officer should be the expert in tactics for non-kinetic maneuver warfare to achieve objectives without kinetic fires. This involves an understanding of decision support, the human elements of adversaries' thinking, language, and culture, and knowing how to use relevant information efficiently. It also involves learning how we assess key nodes for targeted influence operations and a new model for information battle-damage assessment resulting from non-kinetic strikes or activity. Additionally, knowledge managers and their understanding of data structures and human-machine interfaces will be critical to ensuring the tools and processes are in place for technology to assist with the heavy lifting that our brains do now.

Significant predictive computing power exists today, and the formulas used in modeling and simulations to predict environmental effects can be applied to accelerate warfighting decisions and improve the fidelity of information for operational forces.

## Unmanned and Autonomous Systems (UxS)

In accordance with the Department of Defense Fiscal Year 2009–2034 Unmanned Systems Integrated Roadmap, the Navy is increasingly employing aerial, surface, and subsurface unmanned vehicles, or UxS, for persistent maritime intelligence, surveillance, and reconnaissance, signals intelligence, mine-warfare support, strike, and targeting operations, and undersea environmental sensing and mapping. Future versions also will include communications-relay capabilities.

However, in the Navy these UxS systems are being planned, developed, and operated by disparate groups without an overarching strategy to ensure they meet tactical and operational maritime requirements. While some UxSs are intended for kinetic strike, many are non-kinetic information nodes on the global information grid. The cadre working with the UxS drivers from the surface, air, and subsurface communities should take the lead in all aspects of UxS operations.

## Integrating Platforms

Cyber-warfare officers would plan and direct the operational integration of the information capabilities of Navy UxS platforms. As future UxSs are built as modular multimission platforms, the information-warfare commander—now known as the cyber-warfare commander—would work with the strike-warfare, surface, undersea, and air-warfare commanders to coordinate the strike package to be used. Together they would prioritize and execute UxS missions with the cyber-warfare commander taking the lead as the supported commander on all non-kinetic missions that could result in physical destruction. Actual operation of the UxS platforms would be done by trained officers and enlisted from each of the air, surface, and subsurface communities.

Developing and sustaining such officers is not without challenges. A properly developed career path and billet base, from ensign to admiral, would be necessary. The expertise brought by this community must reside on every traditional operational platform, including ships, submarines, special-warfare units, and air squadrons. Officers also would be instrumental on any operational-planning team and in key staff positions. The revised billet base would include opportunities to inject required expertise to ensure command-and-control and operational superiority are effectively executed. For example, the information-warfare commander billet afloat is filled now by many different designators from aviators to IP officers. Standardizing this billet and staffing it with qualified personnel from the cyber-warfare community would yield officers specifically trained in the relevant core competencies. They would combine elements of intelligence, communications, information warfare, influence operations, and oceanography in more effective ways than we do today. Additionally, the initial accession training and educational milestones would require revision to ensure that the modified technical and operational skills needed are inculcated at every level of instruction.

The cyber-warfare community would evolve from its historic support role to an operationally proactive and predictive role. Its officers would be forward-thinking, adaptive planners with superb technical skills, ideally suited to achieve advantages in a disruptive, rapidly changing battle space.

Evolution involves change. As Albert Einstein wrote, "No problem can be solved from the same level of consciousness that created it." As the Navy enters a new military age in which power is not measured by kilotons but by kilobytes, information and the ability to quickly obtain, analyze, manipulate, and correlate data will be the deciding factor for victory. By restructuring our existing officer corps to stay ahead of these challenges, we will be poised to excel in this challenging environment.

# PART IV

## Thoughts on Possible Futures

# 16 "THE TIME FOR LASERS IS NOW"

CDR Bryan McGrath, USN, and Timothy Walton

**In the fourth and final part** of this Wheel Book, we will look at a handful of specific technologies with the promise of significant military applications. The ability to engage a target from great distances, at the speed of light, and at a cost of pennies per "shot" would certainly be game changing. In this article, the authors explain that directed energy and electric weapons (DEEW) may be closer to fleet operators than many believe. They argue that budgetary and organizational decisions must be made *now* to speed these disruptive technologies from the laboratories and onto the steel decks where they are needed.

## "THE TIME FOR LASERS IS NOW"

By CDR Bryan McGrath, USN, and Timothy Walton, U.S. Naval Institute *Proceedings* (April 2013): 64–69.

Prior to the Civil War, a group of innovative leaders touted the value of steam power for ship propulsion. Facing detractors who claimed steam was redundant to the capabilities of sail, or that the technology would only be suitable for riverine traffic, leaders such as Commodore Matthew Perry and later Rear Admiral

Benjamin Isherwood motivated the U.S. Navy to embark on the construction of steam vessels. By the end of the Civil War, the size of the American steam fleet had grown from 28 to 600, and soon thereafter, an increasing number of those were capable of transoceanic travel.[1] By the turn of the century, steam power was essential for a modern naval force.

The U.S. Navy faces a similar situation today, with the technologies of directed energy and electric weapons (DEEW) assuming the place of steam as the disruptive technology. These technologies are rapidly maturing and hold much promise in terms of engagement capability and capacity. Nonetheless, critics view DEEW as redundant to the investments the Navy has made in missile and gun systems, or they assert the technology is not and will not be able to credibly engage advanced threats. The evidence suggests otherwise. DEEW are increasingly capable of engaging much of the spectrum of threats and will greatly add to the Fleet's engagement capability and capacity. Although it is unlikely that DEEW will replace missiles and guns in the foreseeable future, it is clear this new technology can significantly improve a Fleet's defenses and combat potential, diminish adversary advantages, and extend the utility of traditional kinetic weapons systems.

The time is ripe for a new generation of Perrys and Isherwoods to aggressively pursue DEEW technology, define requirements for it, and field it throughout the Fleet.

## Austerity Is the Mother of Invention

Although we live in a proclaimed age of austerity, now is (paradoxically) precisely the time for the Navy to pursue high-technology DEEW systems. In the years between the World Wars, shrinking budgets forced the Navy to think innovatively. The result was a Fleet that valued experimentation, creativity, and technology insertion—one that was ready intellectually to deal with the challenges of World War II, albeit without the force structure to do so. Faced with shrinking budgets, the Navy must optimize readiness and capabilities development. Where it does look to develop new capabilities, it should focus increased attention and resources on those technologies capable of placing the United States on the advantaged side of cost-exchange ratios.

China, the pacing threat, has developed a sophisticated and deep arsenal of precision-guided munitions that threaten to overwhelm our force's expensive and in-short-supply defenses. DEEW systems such as lasers, electromagnetic railguns (EMRG), and high-powered microwave weapons are counter–anti-access/area-denial (A2/AD) capabilities that would contribute to mitigating, and perhaps reversing, the cost exchange. These new capabilities would improve Fleet defenses, allow the Fleet to increase its time on station (fewer reloads), and dedicate kinetic interceptors to stressing targets and to other mission requirements, such as antisurface warfare, antisubmarine warfare, or strike.

DEEW operate on different physical principals than their gunpowder- and high-explosive-based predecessors. This article focuses on lasers, even though many of the principles and challenges faced by introduction of lasers into the Fleet are common to other DEEW systems. There are a variety of lasers, with the most common, contemporary, developmental systems being chemical lasers, free-electron lasers (FEL), and solid-state lasers. Chemical lasers have been tested for several decades, including on the U.S. Air Force's now-canceled Airborne Laser Test Bed. Chemical lasers use a variety of expensive and corrosive chemicals, which impose significant logistical and safety demands. Free-electron lasers use a relativistic electron beam as the lasing medium. Although they hold tremendous promise of capabilities in the megawatt class, the technology requires comparatively more investment and time to mature when compared with solid-state lasers.

## Adding Defensive Flexibility

There are two types of solid-state lasers. Solid-state fiber lasers combine the beams from multiple diodes to create a uniform laser beam. By combining the output of thousands of fibers, high-energy outputs can be achieved. However, due to increased loss in beam quality, they face the limitation that their potential power output is inferior to the other type of solid-state laser: solid-state slab lasers. Solid-state slab lasers, such as diode-pumped solid-state lasers, operate by using a laser diode to "pump" a solid medium. Combining the outputs of multiple slabs is the primary means of achieving higher energy levels. Solid-state slab lasers have achieved a relatively high level of technological readiness (approximately Technology Readiness Level 5–6) and are capable of being increased in power from their current levels, which are capable of engaging subsonic air targets, to levels capable of engaging significant numbers of supersonic ones. In examining its program, the Navy should divide its efforts into the continued long-term research of FEL and the near- and mid-term development and deployment of solid-state lasers.

As a result of their physical properties, solid-state lasers can produce a number of useful effects. Laser optics can be employed for high-resolution target identification and tracking. At low power settings and with coloration, lasers themselves can be used to warn targets at-range. Additionally, lasers could damage certain target electro-optical sensors in order to counter enemy surveillance or to blind missile or unmanned system seekers. Lastly, and most importantly, lasers are capable of destroying targets. Lasers able to deliver adequate irradiance to a target (determined by laser "brightness" or power, beam quality, and stability) for an appropriate period of time can destroy missiles, aircraft, and surface vehicles.

Single ships such as DDG-51 Flight II and III destroyers, aircraft carriers, amphibious-assault ships, and DDG-1000 destroyers armed with lasers could effectively employ them for self-defense against unmanned aerial systems (UAS), boats, and lower-end missiles. Sailing on board appropriate battle-group formations, though, lasers could enable powerful, close-in area defense of groups of ships against advanced threats. Evolved Sea-Sparrow missiles or SeaRAM would likely be required for certain threat geometries during large missile raids; however, lasers would be able to economically engage many if not most of the azimuths of threats. Linked by an in-situ, networked battle-management capability, lasers would "deepen" battle groups' magazines of kinetic missiles. Consequently, lasers would add flexibility to a ship's defense. Commanders would have the option of conserving missiles and engaging threats with lasers, which would save long-range missiles for "archers," advanced threats, and challenging geometries.

Lasers would also add resilience to Fleet defenses with a more capable inner-layer area defense. This would:

- Increase ship survivability, particularly in saturation raids
- Allow engagement of late detects (or guided weapons that quickly pop-up in the littorals)
- Reduce communications or track challenges faced by missiles against saturation raids.

Moreover, lasers would facilitate the rebalancing or optimization of ship magazines. Without lasers, a notional guided-missile destroyer is heavily weighted toward an SM-2/6 loadout, with much less SM-3 and Tomahawk land-attack missile capability. Adding lasers allows a ship to carry a more even distribution that can maximize time on station, ballistic-missile defense, antisurface, anti-submarine, or strike capability. Again, DEEW should not be seen as a replacement for missiles, so much as a means to extend their effectiveness.

## Lasers: *Not* Star Wars

DEEW such as lasers are oftentimes viewed as fantastic "Star Wars" capabilities that, despite repeated promises, have not reached technological maturity and will not emerge for quite some time. Historically, an inhibiting factor for the transition of lasers into the Fleet has been the dilemma that, due to the technological immaturity of the systems, the "conceptual designs of laser weapons that are scaled for combat effectiveness are too large to be appealing to users; conversely, weapons that are sized for platform convenience generally lack convincing lethality."[2] It is a growing consensus of experts, though, that solid-state laser technology has greatly matured and is now ready for fielding of systems with appropriate platform convenience and lethality in the near term.

Representative of developments, in 2010 the Office of Naval Research (ONR) tested its laser weapon system by engaging four UAS targets flying over water. Guided by Phalanx Close-In Weapon System sensors, the system demonstrated the integration of existing technologies with new ones and showed the real promise of lasers. Shortly thereafter, in 2011 the ONR tested its Maritime Laser Demonstration (MLD) program, consisting of a 15-kilowatt solid-state slab laser. The more powerful MLD achieved demonstrated material kills at moving targets from an underway decommissioned *Spruance*-class destroyer. MLD most importantly has the ability to "chain" together different solid-state slabs with relative ease, producing a weapon capable of destroying realistic threats.

Another criticism of lasers is that they will perform poorly at sea because of environmental effects (such as heavy rain or fog) on lasers. Certain laser proto-types have demonstrated great resilience in maritime environments. For example, MLD withstood actual sea conditions, including 8-foot waves, 25-knot winds, and rain and fog. Furthermore, DEEW would be part of an ensemble approach to Fleet weaponry. Consequently, missiles, electronic countermeasures, and appropriate tactics, techniques, and procedures would be employed when lasers might be less effective.

Additionally, a single-weapon solution would fail to provide adaptability to multiple scenarios or changing last-move dynamics. Instead, lasers should be viewed as a powerful new capability that, like any emerging class of weapons, will be gradually integrated into various platforms over time. As such they will coexist for decades—using novel hybrid operational concepts—with existing weapon technology, including missiles, which are essential for beyond-the-horizon engagement of threats.

## The Path to the Fleet

There is increasing recognition within the U.S. Navy that DEEW systems are beginning to reach maturity and that it is time to begin to field them in the Fleet. Sensing the trend, former Chief of Naval Operations Admiral Gary Roug-head tasked the Strategic Studies Group to examine a topic titled "Maritime Operations in the Age of Hypersonic and Directed-Energy Weapons." In April 2012, the Center for Strategic and Budgetary Assessments released a report highlighting the value of directed energy weapons.[3] And the ONR has requested from industry a technical-maturation program to build one to two prototype laser weapons that can achieve 100-kilowatt output and go to sea for up to six months by 2016.[4] This decision, taken with the support of senior Navy leader-ship, clearly affirms the Navy's interest in rapidly fielding these technologies.

In order to succeed, the Navy needs a lucid and aggressive path for the deployment of DEEW. Such a path should involve three main lines of effort:

| MISSIONS | WEAPONS | BASELINE LOADOUT | ALTERNATIVE 1: MAXIMIZE DDG TIME ON STATION | ALTERNATIVE 2: MAXIMIZE STRIKE CAPABILITES | ALTERNATIVE 3: MAXIMIZE BMD CAPABILITIES |
|---|---|---|---|---|---|
| Anti-Air Warfare | Laser Defenses | 0 | 2 | 2 | 2 |
| | SeaRAM CiWs | 21 (deck) | 21 (deck) | 21 (deck) | 21 (deck) |
| | Evolved Sea Sparrow Missiles | 32 (8 cells) | 220 (55 cells) | 0 | 0 |
| | Standard Missile 2 | 40 | 10 | 10 | 10 |
| | Standard Missile 6 | 34 | 17 | 17 | 17 |
| Ballistic Missile Defense | Standard Missile 3 | 6 | 6 | 6 | 61 |
| Anti-Surface Warfare | Anti-Submarine Rockets | 4 | 4 | 4 | 4 |
| Strike | Tomahawk Cruise Missiles | 4 | 4 | 59 | 4 |
| | Multiplier | Baseline | ×12 Time on Station | ×15 Strike Capacity | ×10 BMD Capacity |

- Defining requirements for DEEW through rigorous analysis
- Improving DEEW experimentation and technical maturation
- Optimizing Navy organizations for DEEW.

For DEEW to flourish, the Department of Defense must first define an operational requirement that realistically creates space for a DEEW option to fill. As Distinguished Engineer for Directed Energy and NAVSEA Technical Warrant for Directed Energy and Electric Weapon Systems Dr. David Stoudt contends:

> The continuing problem is matching those unique capabilities to vetted operational requirements. The DE technical community has made great strides in helping the operational community understand the capabilities of DE weapons and their potential military effects on targets. The lack of formal requirements, however, has yielded more of a technology push—rather than an operational pull—of various DE capabilities.[5]

This lack of a formal requirement continues even though there clearly are capability, capacity, and affordability challenges for U.S. naval forces. For example, even though it is common knowledge that in a counter-A2/AD campaign, ships would lack magazine depth for extended operations, current requirements analyze the situation per individual engagement, not at the campaign level. Hence, in a perversion of the requirements process, there is no "gap" to trigger material development, even though there are major existing gaps against both individual threat types and campaign-level aggregations of threats. Definition of these requirements through Navy analysis and the contribution of relevant combatant-command inputs on gaps is an important first step for fielding DEEW.

## Decision Time

Subsequently, the Navy should pursue making a material-development decision (MDD) to address current capability and capacity gaps. An MDD would, based on the maturity of the technology, identify the capability gap lasers would address and recommend the use of an acquisition process to address it. Such a decision would not commit the Navy to fund a laser, or bind it to any specific time lines. However, it would allow Navy offices to investigate material-solution options through an analysis of alternatives (AoA). This would:

- Determine what type of weapon, kinetic or DEEW—and if DEEW, what power and brightness—is best suited to address challenging gaps
- Would allow technology development to continue
- Allow program planning to take place.

A second line of effort for fielding solid-state lasers to the Fleet is furthering experimentation and technical maturation. Both virtual and physical experimentation is needed to refine operating concepts and to refine system-engineering inputs such as lethality and atmospherics. Considering virtual experimentation, modeling experts observe that "conventional air-to-air warfare (AAW) models . . . are not well suited for showcasing current or near-term laser-weapon capabilities" that must engage a target for a period of time, rather than "instantly" destroying it as with a missile.[6]

With regard to physical experimentation, the Navy has faced delays testing lasers, oftentimes due to difficulty reserving adequate range facilities. Accordingly, in order to save cost and speed up testing, the Navy should designate a primary site for experimentation efforts. The Pacific Missile Range (PMRF) in Hawaii provides the perfect location. With high test availability, it allows live fire against all relevant threat types with ready integration with representative radar and combat-system assets. Additionally, PMRF has the space necessary for ready storage of government and industry demonstrators and test equipment. This concentration of advantages would improve efficiency in experimentation and design work and avoid duplications of effort that currently take place. Since the ONR's laser prototypes will not be ready until 2016, the Navy could obtain preliminary test data using the Army's 105-kilowatt solid-state laser at White Sands Missile Range.

## Organizational Inroads

Lastly, the Navy must examine the organizational structures currently in place to field DEEW into the Fleet. A renewal of Navy interest in DEEW has been manifested in the establishment of a number of organizations and positions: the Surface Navy Directed Energy and Electric Weapons Program Office, executive positions and a technical-authority warrant for directed energy, and the Naval Directed Energy Advisory and Oversight Group. These are all very positive steps to leverage DOD's exceptional military and civilian leadership.

Nonetheless, further changes are necessary. To date, no resource sponsor from the Office of the Chief of Naval Operations has been assigned *primary* responsibility for DEEW. A resource sponsor could elevate the prominence of the technology and resolve bureaucratic contention that might arise. Although lasers have important communications and counterintelligence/surveillance/ reconnaissance capabilities, which may suggest a home for them under the Deputy Chief of Naval Operations for Information Dominance, the true scope of their capabilities is more closely aligned with engagement of threats. Consequently, the Director of Surface Warfare should be assigned responsibility for DEEW. Furthermore, if the Navy's AoA suggests a DEEW is the optimal solution for the stated gaps, then an office under the Program Executive Office for Integrated Warfare Systems should logically be formally established to manage the weapon-system acquisition planning and preparation.

These proposed changes in organization are not merely academic. The rapid advancement of DEEW technology over the last few decades, both in the United States and abroad, hints at a shift in the calculus of warfare similar to that which occurred in the interwar period in the early part of the 20th century. Armored warfare, close-air support, carrier strike warfare, and submarine warfare were all made possible by technological advances, but in each case, the countries that made the greatest strides in those new types of warfare were not the originators of the technological advances. Other countries, in particular China, are aggressively pursuing DEEW and may have systems similar in capability to the United States. Hence, we must expect DEEW will threaten its own forces in the future. Additionally, less mature or less bureaucratic militaries may best be able to maximize the impact of novel capabilities by forming new organizations and tactics around them. With several other countries actively pursuing DEEW technology, the U.S. military may be at risk of suffering technological surprise from the very technologies it originally developed.

The Navy today needs a new generation of Perrys and Isherwoods to aggressively pursue DEEW technology, define the requirements for it, and field it throughout the Fleet. Regardless of the age, the Navy's great leaders faced technical, financial, and bureaucratic obstacles that they surmounted. Today's leaders face many of the same challenges with the added rigors of a complex and lengthy requirements-and-acquisition process that forces them to start laying the foundation for a future system long in advance of production. In these times of fiscal austerity, bold Navy leaders must develop those disruptive, game-changing technologies that will win the competitions of the future. As it will take approximately six years from the point of an MDD until the first low-rate initial production system, if the Navy would like to have a capable laser before the end of the decade, and possibly on the first DDG-51 Flight IIIs, the time to act is now.

## Notes

1. Frank M. Bennett, *The Steam Navy of the United States: A History of the Growth of the Steam Vessel of War in the U.S. Navy, and of the Naval Engineer Corps* (Pittsburgh: W. T. Nicholson Press, 1896).
2. Naval Studies Board, National Research Council, *Technology for the United States Navy and Marine Corps 2000–2035: Becoming a 21st-Century Force,* vol. 5 (Weapons), chapt. 6, "Navy and Marine Corps Applications for Laser Weapons" (Washington, DC: National Academies Press, 1997).
3. Mark Gunzinger, "Changing the Game: The Promise of Directed Energy Weapons" (Washington, DC: Center for Strategic and Budgetary Assessments, April 2012), www.csbaonline.org/publications/2012/04/changing-the-game -the-promise-of-directed-energy-weapons/.
4. Spencer Ackerman, "Navy: We're 4 Years Away From Laser Guns on Ships," *Wired: Danger Room,* 30 March 2012, www.wired.com/dangerroom/2012/03 /navy-lasers-four-years/#more-76978.
5. David C. Stoudt. "Naval Directed-Energy Weapons—No Longer a Future Weapon Concept," *Leading Edge,* vol. 7, no. 4 (2012), www.navsea.navy.mil/ nswc/dahlgren/Leading%20Edge/Directed%20Energy/files/inc /1250074754.pdf.
6. Robin Staton and Robert Pawlak, "Laser Weapon System (LaWS) Adjunct to the Close-In Weapon System (CIWS)," *Leading Edge,* vol. 7, no. 4 (2012), www.navsea.navy.mil/nswc/dahlgren/Leading%20Edge/Directed%20 Energy/files/inc/1250074754.pdf.

# 17 "THE RAILGUN ADVANTAGE"

LT Maxwell Cooper, USNR

**Engineers and scientists are now** at work on electromagnetic railguns that may soon be able to routinely hurl non-explosive kinetic projectiles at ranges of over 100 miles and at speeds of up to 4,500 miles per hour. Lieutenant Cooper's article discusses the history of naval gunfire, the degree to which missiles have replaced guns aboard Navy ships, and how railguns could provide a highly effective way to engage lower-end threats at greatly reduced costs. Railguns have the potential to fill existing shipboard magazines with much larger numbers of cheaper and safer projectiles.

## "THE RAILGUN ADVANTAGE"

By LT Maxwell Cooper, USNR, U.S. Naval Institute *Proceedings* (December 2011): 60–64.

United States naval technology has reached a tipping point. The Navy must reconsider the feasibility of high-cost/low-capacity missile technology and begin pursuing low-cost/high-capacity capabilities through new developments in naval gunnery, specifically railguns.

Naval warfare and technological developments have always been interconnected. The navy that dominated was the one best able to expand and incorporate
advanced technologies into its fleet.[1] Naval technology undergoes a predictable
pattern of growth: fleets adopt a technology and build their ships and tactics
around it until a new concept overshadows the previous way of employing ships.
A naval arms race develops until the technology is rendered obsolete or becomes
cost-prohibitive.

Since naval strategists recognized the obsolescence of the ramming bow
and fielded the first practical ship-based guns in the 16th century, the naval gun
reigned supreme as the dominant weapon until the second half of the 20th
century.[2] Admirals understood the defining factor in classifying a ship was not
her speed or survivability but how much firepower she could bring to the fight.
Ships began to be classified based on how many guns they could carry and
were designed to accommodate more. Naval tactics evolved in response to those
technological developments, and the line of battle was developed to maximize
the effectiveness of a fleet's total armament. As guns became larger and more
powerful, naval architects recognized they were approaching the point where
they could not put any more guns on a ship and still consider her seaworthy.

## Transitory Improvements

The race to cram more guns into a single hull peaked in 1852, with the 131-gun
steam-powered HMS *Duke of Wellington*, after which a noticeable decline began
in the number of guns per ship as the exploding shell and moveable turret shifted
the focus from quantity to quality. Those developments prompted ship designers
to think of new ways to defend against them. Ironclads became the new standard. The naval gunnery and armory race continued for almost another 100
years, culminating in World War II with the massive 18.1-inch guns and 26-
inch armor on the *Yamato*-class battleships. As evidence of the transient nature
of naval technology, the *Yamato* and her sister ship, the *Musashi*, were both sunk
by torpedoes and aircraft-delivered bombs.

As that war came to an end and naval weaponry developed, it became
apparent that further research in gun technology was a poor investment.[3] The

limited use of battleships in the Atlantic and Pacific theaters and the emergence of the aircraft carrier and submarine demonstrated that naval technology made possible the shift from capacity to capability. Advances in radar, propulsion, and computer technology offered further capability over capacity. Missile development began to dominate naval strategists' thinking.

This shift was illustrated in 1955 when the USS *Boston* (CA-69) was recommissioned from "heavy cruiser, attack" to the world's first guided-missile cruiser (CAG-1). Appropriately, her aft 8-inch gun was removed to allow for the installation of an antiaircraft missile system. The race intensified to develop more capable missile systems, and developments began to occur so rapidly that older systems were quickly outmoded. In 1968, due to the obsolescence of her missile armament, the *Boston* was reconverted to an attack cruiser and decommissioned two years later.

Just as more powerful guns led to the development of the ironclads, increases in missile technology spawned the development of defensive systems, such as jamming, chaff, and hard-kill missile defensive systems. In each case, as the capability increased, so did the cost. Today, missile development has reached a similar point on the cost-benefit curve as guns did in the postwar period. Further investment, while necessary to keep pace with other missile-based threats and missile defensive systems, has reached a point of diminishing returns.

The Navy has fielded, and in many cases is using, third- or fourth-generation upgrades to missile systems purchased decades ago. These upgrades have been at increasing cost and decreasing quantities. The Navy purchased the Harpoon Block I anti-ship cruise missile in 1977 for $475,000 per unit and later upgraded to the Blk IC. The Blk II was developed during the late 1990s at a per-unit cost of $1.2 million, but the service chose not to purchase the upgrade. In 2006, the Navy considered upgrading the Harpoon Blk IC to the Blk III, which would add a global positioning system unit and data link in an attempt to modernize a 30-year-old weapon for the 21st century. The program experienced cost growth and schedule delays, and the Navy determined the relative increase in capability to be cost-prohibitive and canceled the program. By that time it had already spent more than $110 million in development alone, a number that limited the upgrade to only a fraction of the total Harpoon inventory. The Navy is conducting an analysis to determine the next-generation long-range anti-ship cruise missile capable of meeting 21st-century requirements. Cost estimates are measured in the billions of dollars—before the Navy purchases a single combat-ready weapon.

## Too Rich for the Market

Increased costs result in higher per-unit costs, which drive down procurement numbers. When the Harpoon was first developed, the Navy purchased thousands. Procurement estimates for a replacement system are measured in terms of hundreds. Often this is a result of cost growth and lower budgets.

The same trend can be seen in other defense areas. For example, the Navy canceled the upgrade to the antiaircraft SM-2 Blk IV missile (itself a multigenerational upgrade) in favor of developing the SM-6, albeit at reduced levels. The Navy continues to fund the Tomahawk and its multiple upgraded variants but is also initiating an analysis of a future land-attack weapon. The SM-3 Blk IA ballistic-missile interceptor is due to be replaced by the SM-3 Blk IB, which in turn will be followed by the SM-3 Blk IIA and IIB.

Each successive upgrade or, in some cases, entirely new concept, results in higher development costs, higher per-unit costs, and lower overall procurement numbers. These relatively small inventories force war planners to use expensive and limited weapons only against higher-end targets; the high costs simply make them unsuitable for use against lower-end threats. This has created a gap in the Navy's ability to economically engage lower-end threats such as cruise missile-equipped patrol boats, near-shore undefended land targets, or relatively simple ballistic missiles, all of which could be more economically serviced by a low-cost gun round than by a missile.

Missile technology has evolved rapidly at the expense of cheaper gun systems. The largest naval gun currently in service is the Mk 45 5-inch gun, fitted out on *Ticonderoga*-class cruisers and *Arleigh Burke*-class destroyers starting in 1971. While capable of performing multiple missions, the gun's range is limited to 13 nautical miles, rendering it useful only for self-defense or naval surface fire support. The Navy has attempted to increase the range of the Mk 45 through multiple upgrades as well as the extended-range munitions program, but that was canceled after technical problems, cost hikes, and a series of failed flight tests. The result is 40 years of negligible increases in gun capability.

The Navy is currently developing the Advanced Gun Systems (AGS) for the DDG-1000, a single-mission gun capable of striking land targets at up to 63 nautical miles. This program has also suffered from technical challenges and cost increases, resulting in the truncation of the program from 64 barrels to 6.[4] Other gun systems the Navy is developing offer less range than the Mk 45. The 25-mm, 30-mm, 57-mm, and 76-mm guns all have ranges from between one to ten nautical miles and are for self-defense only.

## The Right Gun for the Job

The lack of a multimission naval gun with a range capable of servicing lower-end targets before they enter a ship's threat envelope forces the Navy to rely on its expensive and limited numbers of high-end cruise missiles for all missions. During the opening salvos of Operation Odyssey Dawn, war planners were required to use Tomahawks to take out all land targets because that was the only weapon available with the required range, lethality, and accuracy, and that did not put any aircraft at risk. In the early stages the Navy launched 124 Tomahawks against land targets. Given Libya's known military capabilities and geography, it is not difficult to assume that the majority of those targets were lightly defended and located within a railgun's projected range. The total cost of these initial strike missions was reportedly $174 million—$1.4 million per missile.[5]

The Navy has recognized the gap in its ability to service lower-end targets at low cost and has pursued the development of short-range multimission missiles. But these have either experienced significant development problems or been canceled because of cost. The most recent example is the cancellation of the non-line-of-sight precision attack munition, a joint Army-Navy program to develop a low-cost/high-capacity missile system for use on both land and in ships. The Navy is investigating alternative options, but given that missiles by their very nature are expensive and low-capacity, it is unlikely an economical missile system will be developed for use against such targets.

Railgun technology can deliver large numbers of rounds over distances comparable to those of most current missiles and with the same lethality and accuracy but at higher quantities and lower costs. Railguns work by passing an electrical current along a set of parallel rails. The resulting magnetic field generates a vector that forces the round through the barrel at hypervelocity. The entire process is driven electrically; no explosive propellant is required. The Office of Naval Research has established a goal of launching a projectile more than 200 nautical miles and recently fired a world-record 32 megajoule shot that equates to roughly half that distance. The round itself relies solely on kinetic energy to provide its destructive power—no explosive warhead is required—and will be equipped with a GPS unit to allow for accuracy over long distances. The lack of an explosive propellant frees space in the magazine for more rounds.

An Mk 45 has a magazine capable of holding 600 rounds and an equivalent number of propellants. The AGS has a magazine of 750 rounds, including propellants, which are integrated into the loading and handling system. A railgun-equipped ship would triple that capacity, and likely more, given that railgun rounds will be smaller than either Mk 45- or AGS-fired rounds.

By combining a railgun's range with a variety of multimission rounds, including air defense, ballistic-missile defense, precision strike, antisurface warfare, and naval surface fire support, a railgun-equipped ship would be capable of conducting long-range missions less expensively and with fewer risks.

For antisurface warfare, a ship could put dozens of shotgun-like dispersing rounds down range that would release their submunitions at the same time, enveloping the target in a massive cloud of shrapnel that would shred its sensors and communications equipment, effectively taking it out of the fight. This tactic would be useful against large-area land targets as well. If the mission called for the destruction of a target in an area where collateral damage was a concern, the shotgun round would be exchanged for a single, larger, and more accurate round designed for precision strike. This would limit collateral damage to below that of a comparable missile as there would be no explosive component. The total cost for conducting these missions would be an order of magnitude cheaper than using current or projected antiship or land-attack missiles. The same theory applies to other missions currently serviced by missiles, including cruise-missile and ballistic-missile defense.

## The Navy's Game-Changer?

It is not difficult to envision a scenario where a railgun would prove itself as the "force multiplier" it is often touted to be. During Operation Odyssey Dawn, the ships involved in the initial Tomahawk strikes were forced to return to port after only a few days on station because they had exhausted their supply of missiles. To ensure that Tomahawks were always available to the theater commander, multiple ships were required to rotate in and out of port. While the exact details remain classified, given that an *Arleigh Burke* destroyer can carry a maximum of 96 missiles and a *Ticonderoga* cruiser a maximum of 126, it would not take long before a single ship had expended its allotment of missiles and have to return to port, especially when one considers that the cells must be allocated between SM-2s, SM-3s, SM-6s, Evolved SeaSparrow Missiles, Tomahawks, and vertical-launched antisubmarine rockets.[6]

By replacing the Mk 45 with a railgun and using that to service the lower-end missions such as airfields, radar stations, and truck depots, and using Tomahawks only against high-end objectives such as command centers or hardened targets, a single ship would be able to accomplish what today requires multiple ships while simultaneously providing greater capability and flexibility to mission commanders.

Railguns also could increase overall ship safety. New missiles are required to travel faster and farther than their predecessors, forcing the development of new types of propellants. As Rear Admiral Nevin P. Carr Jr., former head of the Office of Naval Research, noted regarding ballistic-missile defense, "We're fast approaching the limits of our ability to hit maneuvering pieces of metal in the sky with other maneuvering pieces of metal."[7] (From a cost perspective, this may be a good thing, as the SM-3 Blk 113 interceptor has a per-unit cost of $13 million.)

Most recently, liquid-fueled boosters and hypergolic-based warheads are being explored to provide the required range, speed, and accuracy. These developments present a problem for the Navy as liquid fuel and hypergolics pose significant shipboard safety concerns. By comparison, railgun munitions have no explosive component and require no combustible propellant. Given the Navy's emphasis on insensitive munitions and its goal of maximizing shipboard safety while maintaining sufficient lethality, railgun technology seems a natural fit.

As with any new technology, the railgun comes with significant technical risk and potential for increased expense. The Senate Armed Services Committee, which canceled all railgun research and development funding in the National Defense Authorization Act for FY12, said power generation and bore life, both of which have made significant progress and are no longer considered "show stoppers," remain problems that must be resolved. However, once initial development is complete (the cost of which likely will be equivalent to any new single-mission missile system), procurement costs will be far less than those of comparable missile systems.

Lowering the costs of missiles is difficult not only because they are expensive to develop, but because it is not the launcher that drives up the cost, it is the missile itself. Because of their complex nature and relatively small quantities, missiles do not take significant advantage of economies of scale. The costs do not significantly decrease the more you buy, at least not at the rates the Navy can afford to buy them. The economics of guns are the opposite. With guns the cost is the launcher, not the rounds. Once the launcher is developed, the rounds will be able to be produced in large quantities and at low cost, allowing the Navy to purchase far more railgun rounds than it could comparable missiles.

The Navy has already invested significant resources into the development of a railgun launcher and proved the feasibility of the technology. Combined with the advances that have been made in bore life, power generation, and ship integration, many believe the Navy could equip a ship with a railgun before 2020.[8] By contrast, next-generation missiles for both antiship and land attack are not expected to be fielded until the mid to late 2020s.

The time is right for naval gunnery to come back into vogue. Railguns can fill the gap created by overdependence on missiles and provide future ships with a low-cost, high-capacity, multimission capability that can be employed as an adjunct to high-cost, low-capacity, single-mission missiles. As then-Chief of Naval Operations Admiral Gary Roughead noted, "You're beginning, maybe, to see the end of the dominance of the missile. . . . There may still be some applications that come into play that you might want to use them in."[9]

Just as naval strategists once recognized the inevitability of the gun over the ramming bow, the moveable turret and exploding shell over the broadside, and the guided cruise missile over the conventional gun, so must modern naval strategists recognize the unsustainable nature of the missile race and begin developing an appropriate adjunct capability by investing in railgun technology.

## Notes

1. Roger W. Barnett, *Navy Strategic Culture: Why the Navy Thinks Differently* (Annapolis, MD: Naval Institute Press, 2009) pp. 74–85.

2. R. J. Grant, *Battle at Sea: 3000 Years of Naval Warfare,* (New York: DK Publishing, 2008), pp. 8–13, 30–31, 130–131.

3. MM Stephen Sim, "The Anti-Ship Missile—A Revolution in Naval Warfare," *Journal of the Singapore Armed Forces,* Vol. 2, No. 4, 1998.

4. Ronald O'Rourke, "Navy DDG-51 and DDG-1000 Destroyer Programs: Background and Issues for Congress," Congressional Research Service, 14 March 2011.

5. Tony Capaccio, "Raytheon Missiles Used in Libya Won't Need Replacement Purchases," *Bloomberg News,* 23 March 2011.

6. Norman Polmar, *Naval Institute Guide to the Ships and Aircraft of the U.S. Fleet, 18th edition* (Annapolis, MD: Naval Institute Press, 2005).

7. Spencer Ackerman and Noah Shactman, "Navy Vows to Fight for its Super Laser, Hypersonic Gun," 24 June 2011, www.wired.com/dangerroom/2011/06/navy-vowsto-fight-for-its-superlaser-hypersonic-gun/.

8. CDR Michael Ziv and John M. Johnson, "Electromagnetic Rail Gun: Providing Greater Flexibility for the 21st Century," Office of Naval Research.

9. Spencer Ackerman, "Navy Chief Dreams of Laser Warships, Ocean-Spanning Robots," 25 May 2011, www.wired.com/dangerroom/2011/05/laser-war ships-oceanrobots/.

# 18 "PRINT ME A CRUISER"

LT Scott Cheney-Peters, USNR, and LTJG Matthew Hipple, USN

The **well-known author and futurist** P. W. Singer wrote in his best-selling book *Wired for War* that "perhaps we as a society ought to be paying more attention to the world of science fiction." Examples of fictional capabilities becoming real go back as far as Jules Verne's ocean-ranging submarine *Nautilus* and H. G. Wells' "Land Ironclads" (or tanks) that that predated actual hardware by decades. By the same token, the "replicator" system used in the *Star Trek* movies is shown producing various products on demand, ranging from food to spare parts. As we have seen in other articles in this anthology, reality keeps catching up with science fiction. An article in the March 2013 issue of *Harvard Business Review* was headlined "3-D Printing Will Change the World"—a bold assertion that may prove prophetic. The article goes on to say: "Enabling a machine to produce objects of any shape, on the spot as needed, is ushering in a new era." The concept of 3D printing, or additive manufacturing, is discussed in this article by the authors, who speculate about the degree to which 3D printers (in effect, replicators) may soon be found on every ship and station in the Navy.

# "PRINT ME A CRUISER"

By LT Scott Cheney-Peters, USNR, and LTJG Matthew Hipple, USN,
U.S. Naval Institute *Proceedings* (April 2013): 52–57.

The 3D printing revolution will radically change naval construction and logistics.

It was around 1440 that Johannes Gutenberg unleashed the printing press, an invention that brought exciting new opportunities along with daunting challenges. The press advanced the professionalization of militaries through the use of written doctrine, while at the same time spreading new ideas that helped to spur the wars of the Reformation and Counter-Reformation. More than five and a half centuries later, a new type of printing promises to have similarly far-reaching effects on the world's militaries—specifically, for our purposes here, navies.

Three-dimensional (3D) printing, also known as additive manufacturing, is not just a singular new technology. Where the printing press facilitated the diffusion of new ideas, 3D printing combines the Internet's fast access to information with what *The Economist* calls the "Third Industrial Revolution." While the precise method varies by printer, in general 3D printers build up from nothing to a finalized product, typically by spraying a fill material, layer by layer, from nozzle jets not too unlike those in an inkjet printer. The latter might deliver a faithful recreation of a wrench's one-dimensional image, but a 3D printer can create a metal replica, or even a new wrench. Additionally, unlike a traditional assembly line, it can switch from producing wrenches one minute to gaskets the next.

Companies first put 3D printers to use generating rapid prototypes to test designs. Former surface-warfare officer (nuclear) Brian Jaffe, an MIT student and developer of a 3D printing start-up, estimates that these still account for the vast majority of the machines' usage. But as their capabilities have advanced in the past decade, they have increasingly created finished products. As a result, 3D printing holds the possibility of upending both how and where a whole host of items are produced, with effects on the Navy ranging from ship and aircraft design and construction to logistics to the attendant new challenges that will be generated.

## How to Print a Ship

One of the most immediate ways 3D printing will impact the Navy is through the design and construction of ships, submarines, aircraft, and everything carried on board. This is due largely to the economic benefits derived from the technology.

The initial cost savings of 3D printing come from the designs allowed by the layer-by-layer process. Senior mechanical engineer Peter Schmehl of Maker-Bot, a leading producer of desktop 3D printers, says he believes this process has the potential to "radically change ship construction, making designs that might not be possible using conventional techniques."[1] If the "build volume" is large enough, a manufacturer can print a component as a whole, forgoing the need for further assembly. This means it can go without the brackets, flanges, and surfaces required for handling, bolting, or welding pieces of the component together—thereby saving material and weight. It also means internal systems such as ducting and piping can be designed to maximize fluid-flow efficiency from more rounded shapes, simultaneously eliminating unnecessary system volume and making it lighter still. This is, quite literally, not a pipe dream. As explained in *The Economist*, Boeing already uses "a number of printed parts such as air ducts" in the F/A-18.[2]

Additive manufacturing's second cost savings come from the materials used in the process. The traditional production technique, subtractive manufacturing, starts with a "billet" of fill and whittles it down to the desired product, wasting up to 90 percent of the material. When working with the rare and expensive top-grade materials that the military demands in high-performance aircraft and precision weapons, the waste is all the dearer.[3] Researchers at EADS, a major European aerospace company, found that a type of 3D printing using titanium powder could create parts just as strong as traditionally produced items using only 10 percent of the titanium.

The future of design and cost benefits for the Navy could come from trends toward both the proliferation of relatively inexpensive desktop models and advanced 3D printers with increasingly large build volumes. One professor at the University of Southern California is developing a system to construct entire houses out of large printers using concrete or adobe, and naval ship and aircraft assembly could head toward that sort of all-in-one design.[4] The production lines and shipyards of the future could be, in effect, enormous 3D printers that would maximize the economies derived from the additive manufacturing process. As a further benefit, as long as the fill materials and design files were on hand, Pentagon planners would never need to worry about a particular production line shutting down, since it could be started back up at any time with minimal loss of corporate knowledge.

On the other hand, the spread of cheaper 3D printers could lead to the entrance of a whole new field of competition in the defense sector. Jaffe notes that for now, those able to afford the most capable 3D printers are large, well-established companies and design consultancies, but that new, low-cost models are becoming good enough to compete with the expensive versions. For individuals and small firms with good ideas and the requisite design skills, this should lower the barrier to bid for defense contracts. Industry faces many challenges to realize these promised design and construction benefits, but, to the benefit of the Navy, a good deal of effort will be spent overcoming the problems because of the advantages. The most profound change for sailors could be how 3D printers change normal shipboard operations.

## Basic Shipboard Use

It might be best to leave to industry the job of exploiting *how* this process will change manufacturing, but the Navy should explore capitalizing on the transformation of *where* production can occur thanks to 3D printing. The service would be in good company. In 2012 the Army shipped a 3D printer to Afghanistan as part of its Expeditionary Lab–Mobile, and "NASA has begun projects aimed at creating 3D printers capable of working in microgravity for use in the International Space Station, manned trips to Mars, and even 3D printing of satellites in orbit," Schmehl says.[5] For the Navy, the greatest immediate potential is in the less-exotic field of logistics.

Augmenting shipboard supply departments with 3D printers can alleviate the need to carry large stocks of pre-manufactured stores. Instead of spending weeks trying to track down a repair part or seldom-used consumable, a repair-parts petty officer could scan the discarded part labeled with a barcode, quick response (QR) code, or some other embedded identifier that, once scanned, sends the item's schematics to queue at the nearest printer.

This simple scenario illustrates many potential benefits. The most obvious is the speed with which a ship could secure a replacement part. This is especially true of rare components or those with low-failure rates not typically carried on board vessels or not in large numbers. "An individual ship has hundreds of thousands of parts," says Jaffe, "supply can't stock all of them. For those parts where there are only three in the world a 3D printer would be pretty nice, even if on just one ship in a strike group."[6]

The next improvement is the space and weight saved by not carrying as many of the medium-failure rate items, relying instead on what Schmehl calls the "object on-demand" aspect of 3D printers. Of course fill material will be required, but the Navy can experiment to determine the optimal amount and mix to carry on board to minimize weight. Further, since the materials will be in liquid or powder form, they can be stored in configurations that reduce excess void space from oddly shaped finished pieces and the packaging that protects them.

Two additional advantages come from combining this manufacturing process with information systems. The first, as discussed earlier, is the preservation of knowledge. There need be no worry about the loss of knowing how to build a widget when its maker goes out of business; that data can be simply stored as a design file. However, the Navy may need to experiment with determining the appropriate type of business contract for items when it is no longer purchasing a finished product. Should the design be bought outright? Or should a per-use licensing arrangement be reached, with a clause either securing the rights or paying a company's creditors in the event of bankruptcy?

The second benefit of 3D printers working with existing information systems is the ability to deliver rapid design upgrades to the Fleet. If a critical vulnerability is fixed or new capability introduced, a physical upgrade is possible without waiting to return to port or for a drawn-out supply-chain delivery.

## Room for Experimentation

Printing replacement parts also highlights what should be one of the first goals of experimentation: determine which items it makes sense to print. For the foreseeable future, mass-producing things such as high-use consumables will remain less expensive. There are also limitations on what can currently be printed, and how quickly. For these reasons, it is unlikely sailors will soon line up next to a 3D printer every time they need a roll of toilet paper or fluorescent light tube.

One factor to consider when determining the proper mix of fill materials to carry on board is that every ship and sub may not need the rare-earth metals required to create permanent replacements for higher-end pieces of equipment. But an emergency swap-in that gets a system to 90 percent in the meantime, built from common materials, could be invaluable.

This points to another major initial goal: establishing a process for quality assurance. The Navy will need to determine who verifies that a printed copy meets military specifications, and how. Could a part's design file be preapproved for all copies, or would each copy need individual approval? Would every printer require separate approval to print each type of part? The Navy will need to ensure the 100th copy is just as up to spec as the first. And for those emergency swap-ins, the Navy could explore using a form of the approval process for departures from specifications (DFSs) to set how long and under what conditions the part can be used.

Other questions the Navy must examine include determining the types of printers to procure, how large they should be, where they should be installed on ships, whether every ship needs one, who will create and maintain the parts design files, and what skills are needed to operate and maintain the printers or to assemble printer-produced components to make complete items.

## Redesigning the Logistics Tail

The answers to the questions 3D printers pose will continue to evolve over the years as challenges are overcome and new possibilities and opportunities arise. While the near-term supply scenario sketched here may seem radical, the potential mid- to long-term uses will appear even more so.

Advances in printing and robotics indicate how shipboard additive manufacturing may be useful beyond simple repair parts. Already researchers at the University of Southampton have successfully printed an entire working unmanned aerial vehicle, except for the engine.[7] Meanwhile, this year scientists at the Naval Research Laboratory will start testing on the ex-USS *Shadwell* of the Autonomous Shipboard Humanoid (ASH) firefighting robot, meant to be able to "walk in any direction, keep its balance at sea, and go through narrow passageways and up ladders."[8] The Navy has also funded a similar project at the Georgia Institute of Technology for a "MacGyver Bot" that can solve complex problems and assist in dangerous situations by using whatever it finds nearby.[9] If these trends are a clue, the future could hold the ability to print complete replacements of the robotic crew members, weapon systems, and remotely piloted or autonomous vehicles that fight the ship and project power.

For human crew members, 3D printers might also bring radical changes. Scientists have successfully printed living tissue, and biomedical engineers "in about a dozen major university and corporate laboratories" are working to advance the ability.[10] The result could be extraordinary new emergency medical capabilities available in a ship's sick bay or strike group, including custom-made replacement skin, organs, and bones, with no risk of host rejection by repurposing and replicating a patient's own cells.

Additive manufacturing might even shake up galleys and repair lockers. Specialty printers can create chocolate cupcakes and could in the future displace the 21-Day Menu with on-demand orders. The ability to make custom items could likewise be ideally suited for the demands of shoring and patching during damage control.

Undergirding these advances is the potential to move the point of production from a factory to somewhere much closer to the sailor who needs it. These new printers still rely on a logistics tail to supply their fill materials. Yet even resupply could be augmented or supplanted by machines refilling material stocks from shipboard recycled waste, or the developing concept of biomining—harvesting resources from the surrounding seas or ashore—perhaps with purpose-built 3D-printed vehicles.

These longer-term possibilities will drive more questions and room for Navy experimentation. Conveniently, they also bring the discussion back to thoughts of ship design. Should printers be integrated into it, or should open space be left for embarking the best models? And should systems that support the printers be built into the ship? We need to know whether 3D printers can take advantage of modularity, on which ships it makes sense to include special medical printers, which vessels should have material-harvesting or waste-recycling capabilities, and whether new classes of supply vessels should be dedicated to biomining.

## The Road Ahead

Most of these ideas are visions of the future, in some cases quite far off, should they ever really come to pass. Along the way there are many challenges for industry and the Navy to overcome to take full advantage of additive manufacturing.

As noted, the most capable machines, such as those that can print titanium alloy objects, are, according to Schmehl, "quite expensive and quite large," and increasing the speed of printers is "daunting." However, the competitive effects highlighted by Jaffe should drive down both costs and printing time. Schmehl predicts that "printers will continue to get faster and faster," moving ever-closer to providing true "object on-demand" capabilities.[11]

The costs of fill materials can be similarly prohibitive. This has been due in large part to the proprietary nature of the fill materials and requirements for interfaces with the machines, "just like inkjet and laser printers," says Schmehl, in what Jaffe calls "the razor and shaving blade" model. Movement toward common technological standards and competition will help bring these costs down too—trends toward which MakerBot and other inexpensive 3D printers are pushing.

Printers can't yet build with every material. Jaffe reels off a list of accomplishments-to-be: "Flexible plastics, polymers, rubbers, wax, translucent materials, and different types of metals."[12] He also notes that one of the biggest prizes is being able to combine various materials, mixing mediums all at once or in one machine, to produce more useful and complete items such as motors and circuitry.

Jaffe explains that objects created layer by layer rather than through a traditional casting or molding process are different at the molecular level. This allows designers to develop intricate internal structures that yield stronger-than-normal materials and equipment. But it also leaves some of the cheaper products, like those made with plastics, weaker, because they were not created as individual pieces. This need not remain the case, but it is so now.

Just as Gutenberg's press helped disseminate information more widely, 3D printing brings to America's competitors the same opportunities it brings to the Navy. It introduces new security challenges in efforts to prevent proliferation. In late June 2012, a Wisconsin engineer made headlines when he used a 3D printer to fashion a working receiver assembly for a firearm modeled on the AR-15.[13] Although it was only a portion of the weapon, the project to create a complete gun continues with new supporters. It is not difficult to imagine the attraction of such a capability for some not-so-nice state and non-state actors.

As the Navy introduces 3D printers into the Fleet, it will need to secure them against cyber threats as it does other information systems. Unique vulnerabilities exist from the same 3D printers that are opportunities for our own cyber efforts. For example, a printer could be hijacked to create a self-destructing weapon or an infiltrating robot. Exploitable, unnoticeable design flaws could be introduced, or a crucial supply capability could simply be shut down.

It will take years, likely decades, to overcome all these challenges. But they will not stop the development and evolving opportunities afforded by 3D printers. One of the biggest tasks for the Navy will be to evaluate each new breakthrough's impact on the shifting economic calculus of consigning any one of the thousands of shipboard parts to print-on-demand status. Better understanding of the link between printer developments and new capabilities will allow the Navy to focus research resources to achieve them. The potential cost and capability benefits are enormous. Let the great experiment begin.

## Notes

1. Cheney-Peters interview of Peter Schmehl, email, 29 October 2012.
2. "Solid Print," *The Economist,* 21 April, 2012, www.economist.com/node /21552892.
3. Ibid.

4. Rebecca Boyle, "Giant 3D Printer to Make an Entire House in 20 Hours," *Popular Science,* 9 August 2012.

5. Zach Walton, "The Army Is Deploying 3D Printers to Afghanistan," WebProNews, 12 August 2012.

6. Telephone conversation between Cheney-Peters and Brian Jaffe, 25 October 2012.

7. Clay Dillow, "UK Engineers Print and Fly the World's First 3D-printed Aircraft," *Popular Science,* 28 July 2012.

8. Al Kamen, "Of Machines and Men, and Fires and Fastballs," *Washington Post,* 10 October 2012.

9. "U.S. Navy Funds 'MacGyver' Robot that Can Create Tools," BBC News, 10 October 2012, www.bbc.co.uk/news/technology-19902954.

10. Robert Lee Hotz, "Printing Evolves: An Inkjet for Living Tissue," *Wall Street Journal,* 18 September 2012.

11. Cheney-Peters interview of Peter Schmel.

12. Telephone conversation between Cheney-Peters and Brian Jaffe.

13. Andy Greenberg, "'Wiki Weapon Project' Aims to Create a Gun Anyone Can 3D Print at Home," *Forbes,* 23 August 2012.

# 19 "SECRETARY OF DEFENSE LETTER ESTABLISHING THE DEFENSE INNOVATION INITIATIVE"

Defense Secretary Chuck Hagel

On **November 15, 2014,** speaking at the Reagan National Defense Forum in the Ronald Reagan Presidential Library in Simi Valley, California, Defense Secretary Chuck Hagel announced the new Defense Innovation Initiative. He called it "an ambitious department-wide effort to identify and invest in innovative ways to sustain and advance America's military dominance for the 21st century." He went on to explain: "Our technology effort will establish a new Long-Range Research and Development Planning Program that will help identify, develop, and field breakthroughs in the most cutting-edge technologies and systems—especially from the fields of robotics, autonomous systems, miniaturization, big data, and advanced manufacturing, including 3D printing." In the formal DOD Memorandum that follows he states categorically that "America's continued strategic dominance will rely on innovation and adaptability across our defense enterprise" and refers to this initiative as "a catalyzing effort that will spread and grow throughout the entire Department."

# "SECRETARY OF DEFENSE LETTER ESTABLISHING THE DEFENSE INNOVATION INITIATIVE"

By Defense Secretary Chuck Hagel, *U.S Naval Institute News* (19 November 2014).

Secretary of Defense
1000 Defense Pentagon
Washington, DC 20301–1000
Nov 15 2014

MEMORANDUM FOR DEPUTY SECRETARY OF DEFENSE
SECRETARIES OF THE MILITARY DEPARTMENTS
CHAIRMAN OF THE JOINT CHIEFS OF STAFF
UNDER SECRETARIES OF DEFENSE
DEPUTY CHIEF MANAGEMENT OFFICER
CHIEFS OF THE MILITARY SERVICES
CHIEF OF THE NATIONAL GUARD BUREAU
DIRECTOR, COST ASSESSMENT AND PROGRAM EVALUATION
DIRECTOR, OPERATIONAL TEST AND EVALUATION
GENERAL COUNSEL OF THE DEPARTMENT OF DEFENSE
INSPECTOR GENERAL OF THE DEPARTMENT OF DEFENSE
ASSISTANT SECRETARIES OF DEFENSE
DEPARTMENT OF DEFENSE CHIEF INFORMATION OFFICERS
ASSISTANTS TO THE SECRETARY OF DEFENSE
DIRECTORS OF THE DEFENSE AGENCIES
DIRECTORS OF THE DOD FIELD ACTIVITIES

SUBJECT: The Defense Innovation Initiative

I am establishing a broad, Department-wide initiative to pursue innovative ways to sustain and advance our military superiority for the 21st Century and improve business operations throughout the Department. We are entering an era where American dominance in key warfighting domains is eroding, and we must find new and creative ways to sustain, and in some areas expand, our advantages even as we deal with more limited resources. This will require a focus on new capabilities and becoming more efficient in their development and fielding.

At a time of constrained and uncertain budgets, the demand for innovation must be Department-wide and come from the top. Accordingly, I am directing Deputy Secretary of Defense Bob Work to oversee this effort. He will report back to me quarterly on progress we have made and I will remain actively involved in overseeing all aspects of this effort.

We have always lived in an inherently competitive security environment and the past decade has proven no different. While we have been engaged in two large land mass wars over the last thirteen years, potential adversaries have been modernizing their militaries, developing and proliferating disruptive capabilities across the spectrum of conflict. This represents a clear and growing challenge to our military power.

I see no evidence that this will change. At the same time, downward fiscal pressure will constrain the way we have traditionally addressed threats to our military superiority and demand a more innovative and agile defense enterprise. We must take the initiative to ensure that we do not lose the military-technological superiority that we have long taken for granted.

History is instructive on this 21st Century challenge. The U.S. changed the security landscape in the 1970s and 1980s with networked precision strike, stealth, and surveillance for conventional forces. We will identify a third offset strategy that puts the competitive advantage firmly in the hands of American power projection over the coming decades.

We must accelerate innovation throughout the Department in several linked areas:

- The 21st Century requires us to integrate leadership development practices with emerging opportunities to re-think how we develop managers and leaders.

- A new long-range research and development planning programs will identify, develop, and field breakthrough technologies and systems that sustain and advance the capability of U.S. military power.

- A reinvigorated wargaming effort will develop and test alternative ways of achieving our strategic objectives and help us think more clearly about the future security environment.

- New operational concepts will explore how to employ resources to greater strategic effect and deal with emerging threats in more innovative ways.

- This effort will include many DOD components, particularly, Policy, Acquisition, Technology and Logistics; Intelligence; the Joint Chiefs of Staff; and the Military Departments.

- Finally, we need to continue to further develop our business practices and find ways to be more efficient and effective through external benchmarking and focused internal reviews.

All these areas will be overseen, integrated, and managed by an active and engaged governance structure led by Deputy Secretary Work which will include the Department's senior leaders. Their focus will be to ensure these combined initiatives achieve maximum traction in our system, that institutional barriers are overcome, and that our Department rapidly integrates real concepts and capabilities to improve its effectiveness.

America's continued strategic dominance will rely on innovation and adaptability across our defense enterprise. This will build the foundation for American leadership well into the 21st Century. I consider this a catalyzing effort that will spread and grow throughout the entire Department.

Thank you.
Chuck Hagel

# INDEX

# ABOUT THE EDITOR

**John Edward Jackson** is a senior professor in the Naval War College (NWC) College of Distance Education. He teaches in the area of national security affairs and concurrently serves as program manager for the Chief of Naval Operations Professional Reading Program. A long-time proponent of emerging technology, he has taught one of the college's most popular elective courses, entitled "Unmanned Systems and Conflict in the 21st Century," since the 2009 academic year.

Retiring as a Navy captain in 1998 after twenty-seven years of service in the logistics and graduate education fields, Jackson holds a bachelor's degree in speech and communications awarded by the University of New Mexico (1971), a master's degree in education from Providence College (1976), a master's degree in management from Salve Regina University (1983), and a diploma from the Naval War College (1983). Jackson is also a graduate of the Management Development Program at Harvard University (1997). He is currently on a leave of absence from the doctoral program at Salve Regina University, from which he received a Certificate of Advanced Graduate Studies in 1998.

A recognized expert in the field of unmanned and autonomous systems, Jackson was called to testify before the U.S. House of Representatives Subcommittee on National Security and Foreign Affairs in March 2010.

Jackson has been listed in Marquis *Who's Who in America* since 1997. He is married to the former Valerie Lee McGilton of Huntington Beach, California. They are the parents of two adult children and one unruly Scottish terrier.

**The Naval Institute Press** is the book-publishing arm of the U.S. Naval Institute, a private, nonprofit, membership society for sea service professionals and others who share an interest in naval and maritime affairs. Established in 1873 at the U.S. Naval Academy in Annapolis, Maryland, where its offices remain today, the Naval Institute has members worldwide.

Members of the Naval Institute support the education programs of the society and receive the influential monthly magazine *Proceedings* or the colorful bimonthly magazine *Naval History* and discounts on fine nautical prints and on ship and aircraft photos. They also have access to the transcripts of the Institute's Oral History Program and get discounted admission to any of the Institute-sponsored seminars offered around the country.

The Naval Institute's book-publishing program, begun in 1898 with basic guides to naval practices, has broadened its scope to include books of more general interest. Now the Naval Institute Press publishes about seventy titles each year, ranging from how-to books on boating and navigation to battle histories, biographies, ship and aircraft guides, and novels. Institute members receive significant discounts on the Press's more than eight hundred books in print.

Full-time students are eligible for special half-price membership rates. Life memberships are also available.

For a free catalog describing Naval Institute Press books currently available, and for further information about joining the U.S. Naval Institute, please write to:

Member Services
**U.S. NAVAL INSTITUTE**
291 Wood Road
Annapolis, MD 21402-5034
Telephone: (800) 233-8764
Fax: (410) 571-1703
Web address: www.usni.org